P9-BYR-564

The Creative Pattern Book

Complete Patterns, Intriguing Ideas & Musings on the Creative Process

by Judy Martin

CROSLEY-GRIFFITH
Publishing Company, Inc.
Grinnell, Iowa

Acknowledgments

I wish to convey my heartfelt thanks to the following individuals
and suppliers who helped make this book possible:

Advice and Direction
Steve Bennett, Chris Hulin, Jean Nolte, and Clara Travis

Proofreading
Steve Bennett, Jean Nolte, and Chris Hulin

Quilters
Jean Nolte and Barbara Ford

Quiltmakers
Chris Hulin, Margy Sieck, Ardis Winters, Jane Bazyn, Candace
Carmichael, Karen Cary, Donna Davis, Nancy Mahoney, Elaine
Martin, Jo Moore, Jean Nolte, and Diane Tomlinson.

Photography
Brian Birlauf

Fabrics Provided by:
Benartex
Fabric Sales Co.
Hoffman
Kauffman
Marcus Brothers
Moda
P & B
Springs Mills

Batting Provided by:
Hobbs Bonded Fibers

© 2000 by Judy Martin. All rights reserved.

15 14 13 12 11 10 9 8 7 6 5 4 3 2 1

Printed in the United States of America

Published by Crosley-Griffith Publishing Company, Inc.
P.O. Box 512, Grinnell, IA 50112
phone (515) 236-4854
e-mail info@judymartin.com
web site http://www.judymartin.com

Contents

Patterns

Introduction

An old proverb says, "Give a man a fish, and he eats for a day. Teach a man to fish, and he eats for a lifetime." In the past, pattern books have all been about giving you fish, that is, patterns, on a silver platter, making it inconvenient to make even small changes. After all, changes might alter yardage figures and cutting specs.

My point in writing this book is to empower quilters to express themselves creatively. The Creative Pattern Book is two books in one. Besides having complete patterns for exciting new quilts, it teaches you, by way of colorful examples and clear lessons, how to be creative with patterns. You'll learn easy ways to give your quilt a unique new look and express your personality. You can tinker with color scheme, style, quilting motifs, or Piece 'n' Play arrangements without even having to adjust the pattern. And you'll learn how to use scraps so you won't have to think about yardage adjustments as you play with other elements. You can freely change sizes, borders, and color placement, or add a Smattering of Stars as you make the quilt of your dreams.

The first step in being creative is having the confidence in your abilities to make the quilt you envision. That's why I am sharing with you all my secrets and techniques for fast and flawless patchwork. With just a little practice, you will gain complete confidence in your skills. This will liberate you to concentrate on the creative side of quiltmaking, if that is what you want to do. And if you simply want to make the quilts as presented, that's fine, too. These are strikingly beautiful quilts that you can be very proud of.

Playing (and I do mean playing) with the creative ideas in this book will be fun, and you'll feel a greater sense of excitement and accomplishment from your quilting than you have ever known.

Climb into the boat with me. Together, let's go fishing for the best quilts you've ever made.

Part I
Intriguing Ideas

Small Steps To Creative Quilts. You don't need to be an artist, draftsman, or mathematician to make creative quilts. Simply making a few creative decisions guided by my suggestions will make your quilts unique and personally satisfying. In this section, I'll show you the different effects that result from changing colors, styles, quilting motifs, size, and more. With plenty of color photos for examples, you'll soon learn to "see" quilts in your own fabrics and your own style.

Creative Strides. Perhaps you'll want to go beyond making the usual creative decisions. I give suggestions and show examples of creative touches that you can easily apply to personalize the quilt patterns. I show you how to color outside the block using a design wall, how to add a Smattering of Star blocks for accent, and how to have fun with Piece 'n' Play blocks that can be sewn, then arranged and rearranged for different looks.

Creative Leaps. After seeing the variation among quilts in this book and reading about the creative ideas from which they sprang, you may feel the irresistible urge to take an idea and run with it. I sincerely hope you will feel empowered to give in to your creative impulses, for then you can experience what is, for me, the greatest joy in quiltmaking.

Creative Expressions

a glossary & checklist of ways to personalize a quilt pattern

Size
Add or subtract blocks, borders, or other units to make the quilt larger or smaller

Color Scheme
Choose a different group of colors

Color Placement
Place colors so that different patches share matching colors

Scrap Nuances
Use many fabrics in place of one for tonal variation

Design Wall Coloring
Color the quilt outside the block to form an overall pattern that requires you to lay out units on a design wall or floor

Fluid Colors
Color the quilt so that the whole design flows in and out of colors or values; a kind of design wall coloring

Style
A suite of colors and fabric types that reflects an individual personality or a recognized period or look

Quilting Motifs
Embellish the quilt with interchangeable stitching patterns

Fancy Cutting
Cut patches carefully aligned with a printed motif, such as centering a flower in a hexagon

Staggering
Arrange blocks in stair-stepped fashion rather than in straight rows

Smattering of Stars
Sprinkle the quilt with accent blocks or integrated images such as smaller stars or leaves. These may be placed at regular intervals or at random

Piece 'n' Play
Make asymmetrical blocks, such as Maple Leaves or Log Cabins, and arrange and rearrange them to form a secondary design

Combination
Mix blocks or block elements to create a new pattern

Borders
Adjust border widths or colors or pieced patterns in order to create a new look

Quick-Change Pattern Artistry

Miles of Styles

Adding your own style is the easiest way to personalize a quilt. Whether you prefer cowboy boots, lamé pumps, tennis shoes, or bare feet, your quilt will just naturally be an extension of your personal style. That is not to say that a barefoot quilter cannot make an elegant quilt. Rather, I mean that you have a quilt style just as you have a clothing style. You make style choices every time you buy fabric. So all you really have to do is buy some fabric or look in your stash to see evidence of your style. The fabrics that you choose (and those that you choose to leave out) say something creative about you. Your quilt reflects you whether you try to make it so or not.

Some styles have hit the big time and even have names. Many of these are regional or period styles, such as Amish, Country, or 1930s (or other vintage) styles. You may find fabrics in these popular styles at your favorite quilt shop. Perhaps you have already collected fabrics in a style such as these. You can also tweak these styles with your own fabric mixes.

If your stash has a country twang, your quilt may be very different from one we show in batiks. Don't worry about making such a change; you will surely like the quilt better in your own style. See what a big difference style makes in the Grandmother's Wedding Ring quilts below and the Texas Chain quilts on the facing page. Fig. 1 and Fig. 9 are done in the multicolored style of the 1930s, using reproduction pastels on a muslin background. Fig. 2 and Fig. 4 are done in batiks and contemporary prints reflecting the varied tastes of the quiltmakers. Fig. 3 was inspired by the Amish style. Fig. 5 is in the current style of using just a few fabrics. Fig. 6 is in a Japanese style. Fig. 7 is in the Lodge Look, using flannels. Fig. 8 is in a country patriotic style. The All Star quilt in Fig. 10 is in a vintage 1840s style.

1

2

Quilting Quest

Another easy way for you to personalize a quilt pattern is to choose a different quilting motif for the larger, plainer areas. The Grandmother's Wedding Ring variations on this page are quilted with carnations, feathers, sprigs, and fans for different effects. Grandmother's Diamond Ring (Fig. 1) and Texas Chain (Fig. 8) are both quilted with

3

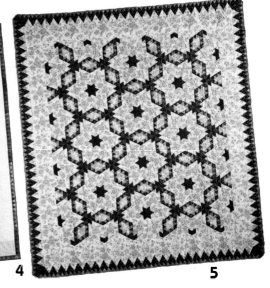

4

5

the same carnation motif. Texas Chain (Fig. 7) and Shakespeare in the Park (Fig. 14 on page 10) are both quilted with concentric circles. Grandmother's Wedding Ring (Fig. 4) and Byzantine Flower Garden (Fig. 19 on page 11) are both quilted with the same sprig motif. You can easily mix and match quilting motifs of similar size. Consider any of the quilting motifs presented with the patterns as well as ones from your own collection. You can also incorporate stippling (Fig. 3 and Fig. 5), or filler grids and stripes (Fig. 6 and Fig. 10) into your quilting plans. Most of these motifs were designed for machine quilting with a minimum of starts and stops, although they look great hand quilted, too.

Color Creativity

Wow! What a difference color and fabric choices can make! Anyone who has ever taken a class and seen the same pattern made up by a dozen individuals in as many color schemes has some idea that the pattern can be just the starting point for a creative quilt. Generally, the first thing that attracts us about a quilt is its color. It is not surprising that many quilters choose a pattern based on its color. Still, this can be limiting. Imagine how many wonderful quilt designs you'd miss out on if you wouldn't consider quilts shown in any color but peach, for example.

Changing color schemes is one of the most rewarding creative touches you can add to a quilt. If you simply substitute colors one for another, it won't render yardage figures, instructions, or diagrams useless. It does take a certain amount of confidence, however. In this book, you can see alternative color schemes that I recommend in other patterns in the book.

This book also shows examples of the same pattern in different color schemes. Figs. 19–20 on page 11 show two examples of the Byzantine Flower Garden in different color schemes. Judy's Maple Leaf (Fig.11 on page 10) and Grandmother's Wedding Ring (Fig. 4 on page 8) show two different patterns in the same color scheme. Studying pictures such as these will

10

9

6

7

8

9

11

help you anticipate how colors affect the look of a quilt. When you see how you are attracted by colors, you'll learn to see past that, and you'll really consider patterns for their other qualities.

Notice the way the stars stand out in the Horn of Plenty quilt in Fig. 15 below. The Horn of Plenty quilt in Fig. 16 on the facing page has stars so subtle that they blend into the background. Stars play a bit part in this version, where diagonal bands of color take center stage. These two variations of the same quilt pattern are examples of changes in color placement. By coloring different sets of patches to match each other you bring out different design elements. In Figs. 6–8 on page 9, notice how the color placement of squares and backgrounds subtly changes the look of each quilt. The two Shakespeare in the Park quilts in Figs. 13–14, below, sport different color schemes and different color placement, as well. The smaller version is interpreted in four colors instead of two. The Grandmother's Wedding Ring quilts on page 8 and the Acrobatik quilts in Figs. 17–18 on page 11 achieve varying rhythms due to changes in color placement.

Changing the color placement can affect yardage in large or small ways. I heartily recommend using a scrap style so that you can simply buy additional fat quarters if you run out of fabric. In order to mix scraps well throughout the quilt, cut the entire quilt before you get too far into piecing. If you need to know yardage adjustments, I recommend *Judy Martin's Ultimate Rotary Cutting Reference,* which lists the number of patches that a yard of fabric will yield for most of the patches in *The Creative Pattern Book.*

As important as color is for quiltmaking, you may be surprised to know that I design my quilt patterns in black and white, not in color. I think of the design as a pattern of light and dark shapes. I don't even think about the colors until I pick the fabrics for making the quilt. You may want to make a black-and-white photocopy of a quilt picture from this book to see it in neutral tones. Stripping the quilt of its existing colors may help you imagine the quilt in your own favorite colors.

12

13

14

15

10

Some quilters take the attitude of the more, the merrier, when it comes to fabrics. When you love fabric, why limit yourself to three fabrics when you can use thirty? Other quilters prefer the less-is-more philosophy. (My husband, who likes the clean-lined simplicity of just a few fabrics, made me say this.) Quilts made from just a few fabrics take less time to cut and require no stash of fabric, but scrap quilts have so many more details to amaze you. They have nuances of color that draw you into the quilt. They can have a brilliant splash of color without going overboard. All of the quick or thoughtful decisions about which patches to place side by side live on in the quilt to tickle the fancy of anyone who cares to look.

I must admit that I have a strong personal preference for scrap quilts, so most of the quilts in this book are shown in scraps. However, they could easily be interpreted in just a handful of fabrics. Yardage listed works for scraps as well as for quilts of just a few fabrics. Acrobatik (Fig. 17 below) is made from scraps. The same quilt is made from seven fabrics in Fig. 18. Five versions of the Grandmother's Wedding Ring quilt are shown on page 8. Fig. 5 is made from just five fabrics. The others are made from scraps.

Scrap looks can be achieved with new yardage or fat quarters. True scraps are not a requirement. Scrap colorations add nuances of shading and dimensionality. They also look personal, unique, and lively. Scrap quilts have been popular forever, so you can use vintage fabrics and reproductions to achieve authentic looks from the Civil War era, the 1930s, or another period.

I enjoy working with scraps because they extend the planning and decision making into the sewing process. The decisions are quick, not monumental, but they make the quilt more personal and unique. I also like the layers of complexity that scraps add.

20

19

16

17

18

11

I used to advocate using scrap fabrics sorted by color scheme or by theme or feeling: clear happy colors with similarly jaunty colors, autumn shades together, and so on. That works fine, but it feels a bit too safe to me now. (I'm a fabric rebel!) While I would not put every color in a quilt, it is hard to say which colors I wouldn't use together. I sort more by style than color. I'll use '30s or Japanese fabrics, for example. I do like a little color tension, tartness, and an element of surprise. Touches of clashing colors provide this. I also like a great deal of variation and nuance. I tend to dance all around a color and avoid overmatching.

Scrap quilts can be made in color schemes, just like quilts from a few fabrics. For each color, however, you use numerous fabrics. Fig. 14 on page 10 is a good example. Scrap quilts can also be made block by block, with a different set of fabrics for each block. Fig. 29 at right is an example of this kind of scrap quilt. Quilts can be made from fabrics sorted into loose categories such as "light" and "dark," as well. Fig. 22 below is a good example. Sometimes, a quilt has assorted scraps and a contrasting background. Fig. 17 on page 11 is such a quilt. Sometimes these scraps conform to a color theme, such as fall colors in Fig. 11–12 on page 10.

21

22

Piece 'n' Play

Piece 'n' Play offers the most fun you can have with a quilt pattern. When blocks are not symmetrical, they can be turned to make different looks. Log Cabin blocks are the obvious example, with their light and dark halves and their numerous setting arrangements. Figs. 21–28 illustrate Log Cabins and other light/dark blocks in a variety of sets. The leaf blocks in Figs. 11–12 on page 10 can also be turned for interesting effects.

For Piece 'n' Play, you simply make the blocks as described in the pattern. Then you play with their arrangement before you stitch them into rows. The blocks and accents of Smattering of Star quilts offer similar opportunities for Piece 'n' Play.

23

24

25

A Smattering of Stars

Any pattern can be enlivened by adding a Smattering of Stars. These stars can be incorporated into the block, they can be separate units interspersed among the blocks, or they can be used in the borders. The Wilderness Log Cabins (Figs. 21–22 on page 12) have integrated stars within some of the Log Cabin blocks. They also have separate stars in the borders. The stars may be placed randomly or in a regular pattern. In Chris Hulin's Judy's Fancy (Fig. 30 at right), small accent stars are placed randomly. In my version (Fig. 29), they are arranged around the perimeter as a kind of border.

30

I first envisioned these accents as stars because I am something of a star fanatic. However, accent blocks of this kind need not be stars at all. The All Star quilt in Fig. 10 on page 9 has a Smattering of Pinwheel blocks in the border. The 9-Patch variation in Fig. 28 below is embellished with Maple Leaves built into some of the blocks.

Simple repetitive patterns, especially, are improved with accent blocks. 1000 Pyramids, 9-Patch, Log Cabin, Rail Fence, Flying Geese, Virginia Reel, and such are well-suited to accent blocks. The Horn of Plenty quilts in Figs. 15–16 on pages 10–11 are based on 1000 Pyramids with occasional stars incorporated into the design. Shakespeare in the Park (Figs. 13–14) inserts Rising Star and Evening Star blocks among Virginia Reel blocks.

In my design work, I often incorporate a star into a traditional block. It breathes new life into an old pattern. My Colorado Log Cabin, incorporating LeMoyne Stars in the corners of Log Cabin blocks, was probably my most popular example. I've been at it again, concocting in my laboratory. There are several patterns of this type in *The Creative Pattern Book.* Grandmother's Wedding Ring (Figs. 1–5 on page 8) combines stars and Grandmother's Flower Garden elements with a Double Wedding Ring idea. Byzantine Flower Garden (Figs. 19–20 on page 11) builds a star into the center of a Grandmother's Flower Garden-inspired unit. Follow my patterns or, if you prefer, consider building a star into your favorite block for a creative new design.

29

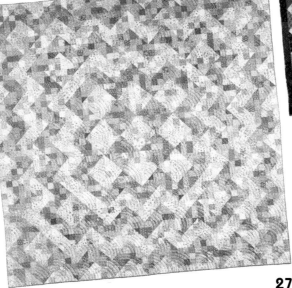

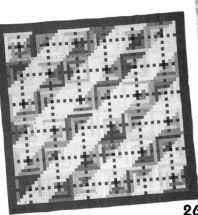

26

27

28

13

Sizing Secrets

Quilters of all skill levels routinely change a quilt's size without much trepidation. Size changes don't take too much creativity: you simply make more or fewer blocks and rows. If you use scraps, you won't have to worry about changes to the yardage figures. Just keep cutting scraps until you have enough blocks. Remember that borders, backgrounds, linings, and bindings, too, can be made from scraps. In fact, scrap borders and linings often save considerably on yardage, as they need not be seamless lengths.

I do a great many calculations for the yardage and cutting specifications in my books. And I enjoy doing the math. However, I don't do these calculations until after I have made the quilts. In my own quiltmaking, I like to simply make blocks until the quilt feels finished. Feel free to do the same yourself.

Some of the quilts in this book are made from triangular or hexagonal units rather than square blocks. Size changes for these quilts can be accomplished by adjusting the number of rows and the number of units per row.

Size changes may affect the widths as well as the lengths of borders. Pieced borders will require different numbers of border units. For some quilts with pieced borders, interior plain border strips may need to be cut in different widths in order to fit a different pieced border length.

Size changes will inevitably change yardage and cutting figures. For those of you who like to know precisely where you are going and how much fabric you will need, you will be pleased to know that many of the quilts in this book are presented with size variations. If you don't find the size you want in your chosen pattern, you will find that *Judy Martin's Ultimate Rotary Cutting Reference* will provide yardage assistance.

Bordering on Brilliance

A simple way to alter the size of the quilt without having to do much figuring is to change the border. However, this can change the entire look of a quilt. I don't usually recommend major changes in border width. And I definitely don't recommend adding a plain wide border to save time. It will need heavy quilting (not a quick solution!) to set off the quilt properly.

The Grandmother's Wedding Ring quilts (Figs. 1–5 on page 8) have slight variations in their borders. Fig. 1 has only a wide plain border in a contrasting color. Fig. 2 has a narrow inner border to match the background and a pieced outer border. Figs. 3–4 have wide inner borders as well as the pieced outer borders. Fig. 5 has a wider plain inner border and an additional, larger pieced border inside the outer pieced border. All examples serve the quilts well, don't you think?

An appropriate border is a crowning touch for a quilt. A border's looks are as important as its contribution to the size of the quilt. I designed these quilts with suitable borders. However, the borders shown are not the only ones that would enhance these quilts. Many of the borders here can be mixed and matched. The dogtooth borders, diamond borders, parallelogram borders, and clipped diamond borders from Figs. 2–5 and 15–20 are all based on 60° angles and could be mixed and matched among the Grandmother's Wedding Ring, Byzantine Flower Garden, Horn of Plenty, and Acrobatik quilts. I would recommend adjusting border unit sizes to match the units in the quilt center.

You can also borrow other border ideas from the quilts presented in this book. Fig. 5 has a wide quilted border followed by a narrow pieced border. Fig. 11 has a narrow pieced border followed by a wide quilted border. Fig. 10 has a wide printed border. Fig. 17 has a wide pieced border followed by a narrow plain border. The quilt in Fig. 27 had a narrow plain border, but I removed it before sending it out for quilting. Although most quilts are improved by a border, this medallion-look quilt simply looks better without one.

Part II
Empowering Know-How

Wouldn't it be terrific if your quilts would just fall together effort-lessly? No fussing, no finagling, no easing, no adjustments? Well, help is on the way. People are always commenting on my quilts' crisp points and precise joints. This is not something I work at. It happens simply because I've learned some easy stuff that really works. The techniques I share here blend the best ideas of our quilting forebears with the latest tools to ensure fast and accurate results. Learn how to lay the foundation for success before you take the first stitch. With these tips you'll save time and avoid aggravation. Getting your quilt right from the start could just be the ultimate timesaving shortcut.

I know a woman who took a class to learn how to make a Nine-Patch quilt. She promptly made 15 Nine-Patch quilts. It wasn't that she loved the pattern so much. She simply didn't know how to make anything else. Many of today's classes stress the unique process for making a particular quilt, so it is not surpris-ing that quilters are intimidated by the prospect of trying a new pattern. My goal is to empower quilters, to give them the know-how to make a wide variety of beautiful quilts, and to give them skills they can build on. Unlike strip piecing, my quick methods are adaptable to any pattern. In no time at all you can learn the seven secrets and master the skills that will enable you to successfully make any quilt you desire.

Rotary Cutting: Squares, Rectangles & Right Triangles

Left Handed

Right Handed

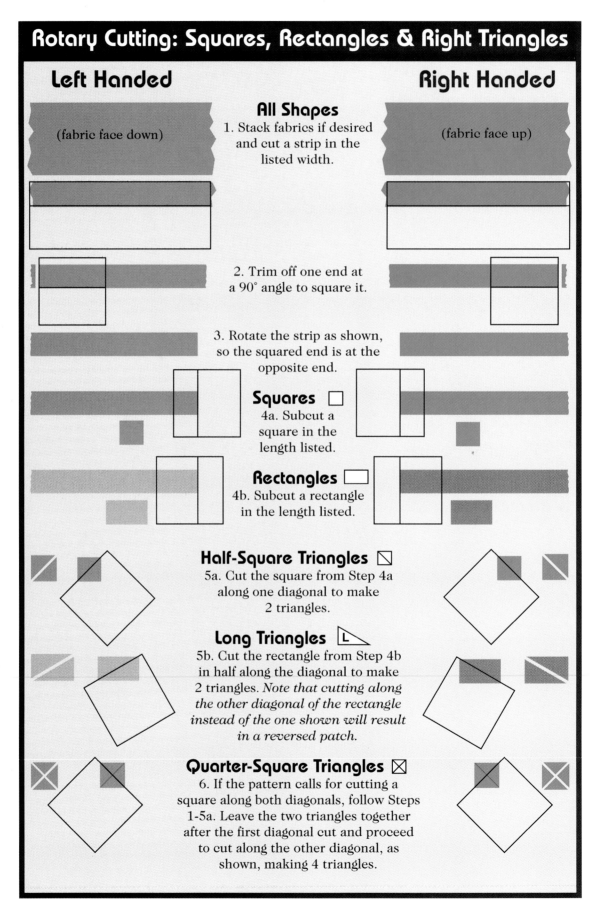

(fabric face down)

(fabric face up)

All Shapes
1. Stack fabrics if desired and cut a strip in the listed width.

2. Trim off one end at a 90° angle to square it.

3. Rotate the strip as shown, so the squared end is at the opposite end.

Squares ▢
4a. Subcut a square in the length listed.

Rectangles ▭
4b. Subcut a rectangle in the length listed.

Half-Square Triangles ◨
5a. Cut the square from Step 4a along one diagonal to make 2 triangles.

Long Triangles ◺
5b. Cut the rectangle from Step 4b in half along the diagonal to make 2 triangles. *Note that cutting along the other diagonal of the rectangle instead of the one shown will result in a reversed patch.*

Quarter-Square Triangles ⊠
6. If the pattern calls for cutting a square along both diagonals, follow Steps 1-5a. Leave the two triangles together after the first diagonal cut and proceed to cut along the other diagonal, as shown, making 4 triangles.

Left Handed

Right Handed

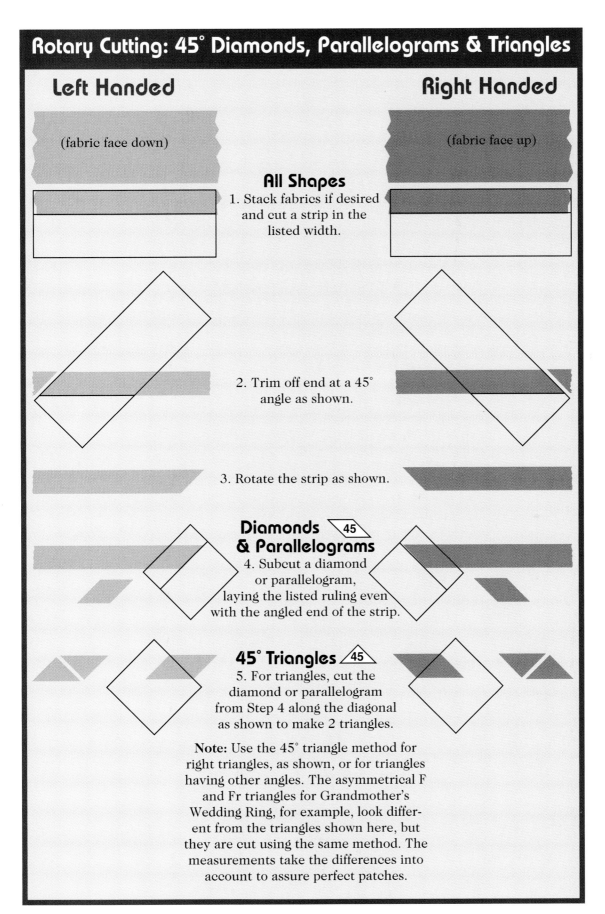

(fabric face down)

(fabric face up)

All Shapes

1. Stack fabrics if desired and cut a strip in the listed width.

2. Trim off end at a 45° angle as shown.

3. Rotate the strip as shown.

Diamonds & Parallelograms

4. Subcut a diamond or parallelogram, laying the listed ruling even with the angled end of the strip.

45° Triangles

5. For triangles, cut the diamond or parallelogram from Step 4 along the diagonal as shown to make 2 triangles.

Note: Use the 45° triangle method for right triangles, as shown, or for triangles having other angles. The asymmetrical F and Fr triangles for Grandmother's Wedding Ring, for example, look different from the triangles shown here, but they are cut using the same method. The measurements take the differences into account to assure perfect patches.

Rotary Cutting: Two Methods for Half Trapezoids

Left Handed

(fabric face down)

Right Handed

(fabric face up)

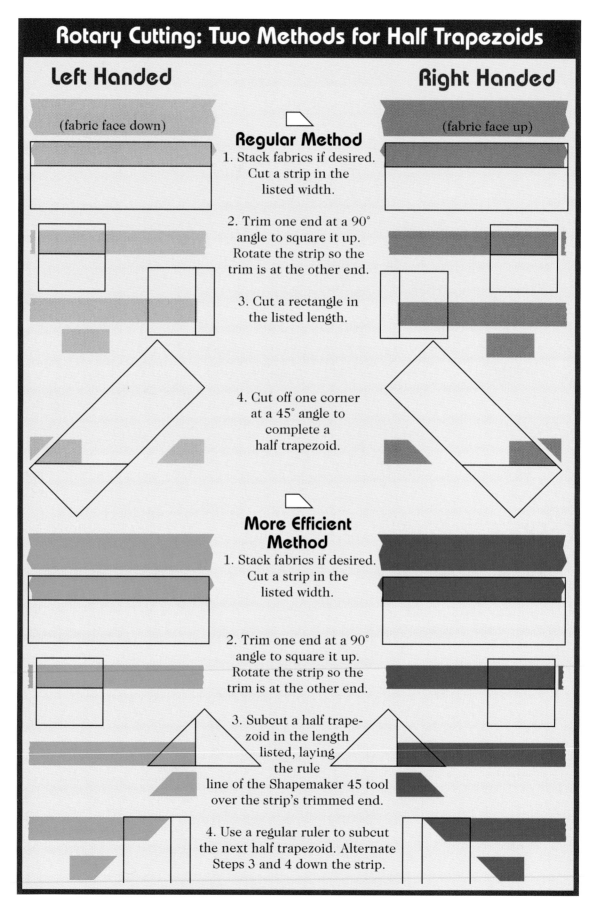

Regular Method

1. Stack fabrics if desired. Cut a strip in the listed width.

2. Trim one end at a 90° angle to square it up. Rotate the strip so the trim is at the other end.

3. Cut a rectangle in the listed length.

4. Cut off one corner at a 45° angle to complete a half trapezoid.

More Efficient Method

1. Stack fabrics if desired. Cut a strip in the listed width.

2. Trim one end at a 90° angle to square it up. Rotate the strip so the trim is at the other end.

3. Subcut a half trapezoid in the length listed, laying the rule line of the Shapemaker 45 tool over the strip's trimmed end.

4. Use a regular ruler to subcut the next half trapezoid. Alternate Steps 3 and 4 down the strip.

Rotary Cutting: Two Kinds of Kites

Left Handed   30° Kites for Borders 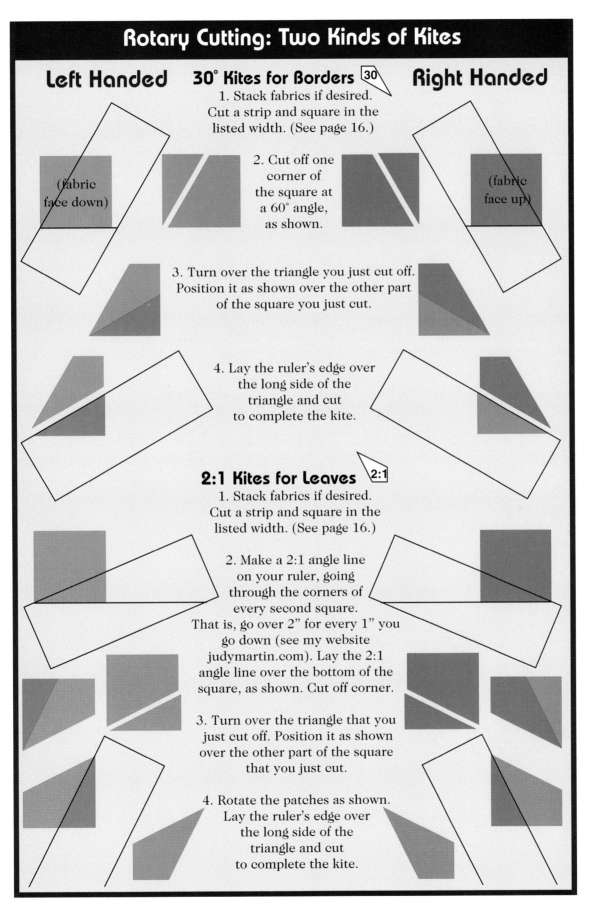   Right Handed

1. Stack fabrics if desired. Cut a strip and square in the listed width. (See page 16.)

(fabric face down)

(fabric face up)

2. Cut off one corner of the square at a 60° angle, as shown.

3. Turn over the triangle you just cut off. Position it as shown over the other part of the square you just cut.

4. Lay the ruler's edge over the long side of the triangle and cut to complete the kite.

2:1 Kites for Leaves

1. Stack fabrics if desired. Cut a strip and square in the listed width. (See page 16.)

2. Make a 2:1 angle line on your ruler, going through the corners of every second square. That is, go over 2" for every 1" you go down (see my website judymartin.com). Lay the 2:1 angle line over the bottom of the square, as shown. Cut off corner.

3. Turn over the triangle that you just cut off. Position it as shown over the other part of the square that you just cut.

4. Rotate the patches as shown. Lay the ruler's edge over the long side of the triangle and cut to complete the kite.

19

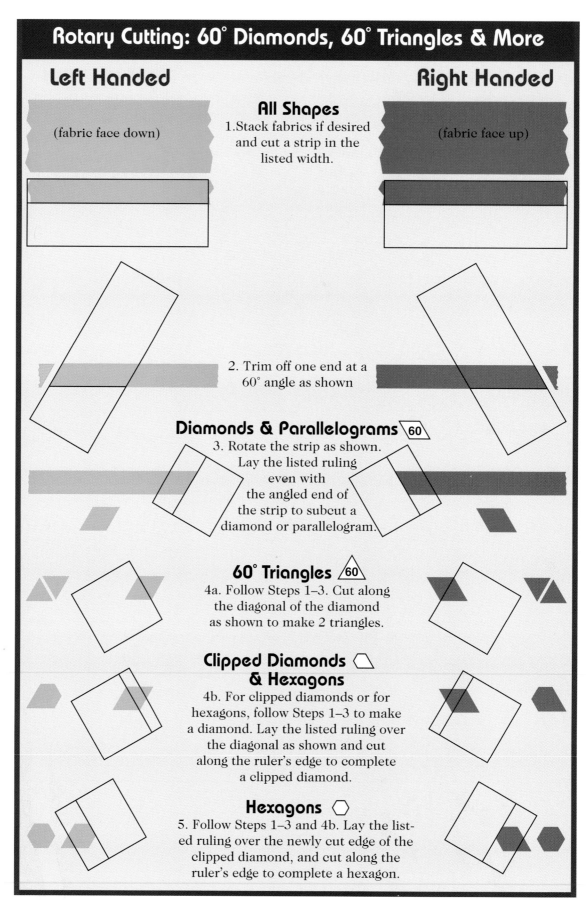

Left Handed

Right Handed

(fabric face down)

(fabric face up)

All Shapes
1. Stack fabrics if desired and cut a strip in the listed width.

2. Trim off one end at a 60° angle as shown

Diamonds & Parallelograms
3. Rotate the strip as shown. Lay the listed ruling even with the angled end of the strip to subcut a diamond or parallelogram.

60° Triangles
4a. Follow Steps 1–3. Cut along the diagonal of the diamond as shown to make 2 triangles.

Clipped Diamonds & Hexagons
4b. For clipped diamonds or for hexagons, follow Steps 1–3 to make a diamond. Lay the listed ruling over the diagonal as shown and cut along the ruler's edge to complete a clipped diamond.

Hexagons
5. Follow Steps 1–3 and 4b. Lay the listed ruling over the newly cut edge of the clipped diamond, and cut along the ruler's edge to complete a hexagon.

Left Handed

Right Handed

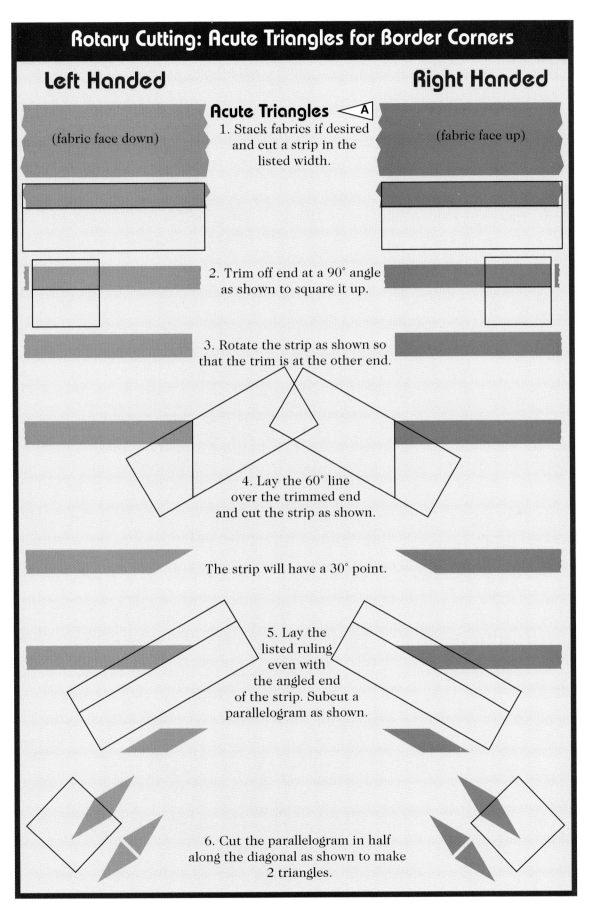

Acute Triangles ◁A

(fabric face down)

(fabric face up)

1. Stack fabrics if desired and cut a strip in the listed width.

2. Trim off end at a 90° angle as shown to square it up.

3. Rotate the strip as shown so that the trim is at the other end.

4. Lay the 60° line over the trimmed end and cut the strip as shown.

The strip will have a 30° point.

5. Lay the listed ruling even with the angled end of the strip. Subcut a parallelogram as shown.

6. Cut the parallelogram in half along the diagonal as shown to make 2 triangles.

Reverse Psychology

Most of the common patches, such as squares and rectangles, are symmetrical; that is, they look the same face up or face down. These can be cut right or left handed, with fabric folded in half or not, with the same results. Some other patches, such as long triangles, parallelograms, and half trapezoids, are asymmetrical. Take special care to cut these asymmetrical patches according to your quilt plan.

Rotary Cutting Reversals

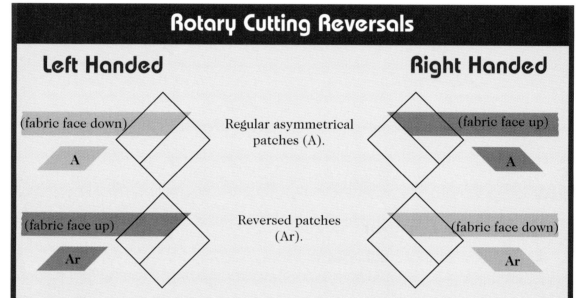

Left Handed   Right Handed

(fabric face down) — Regular asymmetrical patches (A). — (fabric face up)

A   A

(fabric face up) — Reversed patches (Ar). — (fabric face down)

Ar   Ar

Here are some helpful guidelines:

1. Some quilts call for asymmetrical patches and their reverses in equal quantities. These are mirror images; cut both at the same time from fabric folded in half.

2. Mirror images can also be cut from stacked fabrics, half of them face up and half face down.

3. Sometimes all asymmetrical patches in a quilt are alike. In such a case, you must not fold the fabric. Furthermore, care must be taken to keep stacked fabrics all facing the same side up.

4. If your quilt calls for asymmetrical patches that are the reverse of the ones shown on pages 16–21, turn the fabric over (switch face down for face up and vice versa). That is, right handers turn the fabric face down and left handers turn the fabric face up. Do everything else just as the drawings show.

Simply Sixteenths

In the past, sixteenths didn't come up much. Sometimes, numbers were merely rounded to the nearest eighth (!), and sometimes designs were avoided if they had sixteenths. A glance through the cutting specifications in this book will show just how many useful patch shapes and sizes can be cut when you know how to cut sixteenths.

Quilters are more accustomed to eighths than sixteenths. Most rotary rulers do not indicate sixteenths. Sixteenths fall halfway between two neighboring eighths. In this book, ¹⁄₁₆ inches are designated the way you would use your ruler to cut them. That is, the book lists the next lower eighth followed by a "+." For example, 1¹⁄₁₆" would be 1+".

My Rotaruler 16 (R16) is the only ruler to allow you to cut sixteenths following a rule line. In addition to the standard rulings at ¹⁄₈" intervals, the R16 has complete rule lines for ¹⁄₁₆" intervals without the clutter of additional lines. This is accomplished by adding ¹⁄₁₆" to the outside edge on two adjacent sides of the ruler. Cutting along the clear edges gives you ordinary measurements. Cutting along the black edges, yields measurements that are ¹⁄₁₆" larger. You must pay attention to which edge you cut along when you use this ruler, but you will quickly learn to watch for the heavy black line.

Rotary Cutting Sixteenths

Regular Ruler

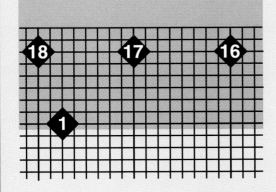

Sixteenths can be cut using an ordinary ruler simply by placing the fabric edge halfway between the eighth listed and the next higher eighth. Here, the lower edge of the fabric is halfway between 1" and 1⅛". This strip would be 1¹⁄₁₆" wide, and it would be listed in this book as "1+".

Rotaruler 16 (R16)

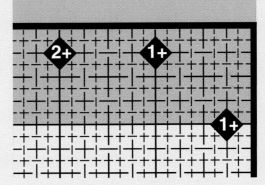

The Rotaruler 16 (R16) allows you to cut sixteenths following a rule line. Cutting along its black edge adds ¹⁄₁₆" to your measurements, and you simply follow the rule line for the next lower eighth. For example, 1¹⁄₁₆" is called "1+," and you follow the R16's rule line labeled "1+."

7 Secrets of Sewing Success

1. Go with the Grain

Fussing, finagling, and fighting with the patches is not my idea of fun. I prefer to piece when I have set the scene for success by going with the grain. When you let the straight grain do its job, you can handle your blocks and units without having to worry about stretching their edges. Think of it as a matter of being a good boss. As a boss, you can delegate responsibilities. You can say, "Straight Grain, it's your job to make sure my patches don't stretch." Your work will be easier and the results better.

To put straight grain around the edges of the blocks and sub-units, simply follow the cutting directions in my patterns. My cutting directions rely on lengthwise grain rather than the more common crosswise grain, giving you the most stable, least stretchy patches you have ever pieced.

You can even press to your heart's content when your units have straight grain all around them. Don't let the bias boss you around. Go with the grain, and be your own boss! You'll be glad you did.

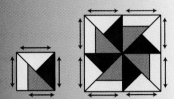 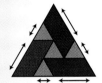 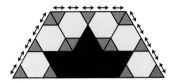

place straight grain around edges of units and blocks

2. The Long & Short of Lengthwise Strips

It's time for one of those lessons of history that are designed to keep us from repeating our mistakes. The Dark Ages weren't so-named because quilters preferred indigoes and burgundies over pastels or jewel tones. No, the Dark Ages were a time in Europe when much of classical knowledge and the wisdom of ancient Greece and Rome was forgotten, lost to most of the people. Then, during the Renaissance, people "rediscovered" knowledge that had been there all along.

Well, quilting is in a Golden Age, a renaissance. But there are a couple of areas where quilters are still in a Dark Age, having forgotten the wisdom of generations of quilmakers who came before them. One has to do with cutting crosswise strips.

Your grandma would marvel at your fancy sewing machine and your rotary cutter and all the wonderful fabrics you have. And then she'd wonder what in tarnation you are doing cutting crosswise strips! If you are not already doing it, the time has come to rediscover the wisdom of your grandma and her peers. Gran would say, "My lands, girl! Lengthwise strips would give you more stable grain. Didn't they teach you that in seventh grade Home Ec?"

Guess what? Grandma would be right. She knows that the lengthwise grain of the fabric is more stable and less stretchy than the crosswise grain. (That's why dressmaking patterns have you align grain arrows parallel to the selvedges.) Grandma also knows that on any fabric, the printed pattern aligns perfectly with the lengthwise grain, but often does not follow the crosswise thread.

Still not sure? Try these tests. Hold a piece of fabric with your hands 6" or 8" apart on the crosswise grain. Bring your hands together, then quickly pull the fabric outward with a snap. Now, repeat on the lengthwise grain. Even with the selvedge removed, the lengthwise grain is significantly firmer, as you will note by the crisp snap on the lengthwise grain as opposed to the dull thud on the crosswise. Now hold the fabric with your hands shoulder width apart, and stretch gently, first on the crosswise grain, then on the lengthwise grain. Note how much more it stretches on the crosswise grain.

Even though many patchwork shapes end up with sides on both the lengthwise grain and the crosswise grain, it is always best to start with a lengthwise strip. For some shapes, such as diamonds, two sides are on the straight grain and two on the bias. Crosswise strips yield a somewhat stretchy crossswise edge and a bias one, whereas lengthwise strips yield a stable lengthwise edge and a bias edge.

Convinced? I thought so. You know what the best part is? You don't have to throw out everything you've learned about rotary cutting. You can start using lengthwise strips today.

How to Cut Lengthwise Short Strips

Lengthwise strips have the long side of the strip parallel to the selvedge. Strips can be any length, but I generally use 18" strips, which can be cut from fat quarters or half yard lengths. Before you layer fabrics and cut strips, trim off the selveges.

You may place the fabric with the long, trimmed edge and lengthwise grain parallel to the front edge of the cutting table, and

cut from right to left or from left to right. This is the method that I use. If you prefer, you may place the fabric with the crosswise grain parallel to the front edge of the table, and cut away from your body.

For a quilt with a scrap look, stack four different unfolded fabrics to make four layers. Because there is no fold, the fabrics lay perfectly flat and are easier to align and cut precisely. Align and press enough of each fabric to cut the needed strips. I sometimes cut just one strip from each fabric. The shorter (18") length of lengthwise strips allows for more scrap variety than 44" crosswise strips permit.

If you will be cutting many strips from the same long yardage, you may cut the fabric into 18" lengths (or any other length up to 24" if you prefer). You can stack the pieces for up to four layers and cut as described above. This avoids folds and keeps your stacks of fabric flat and even.

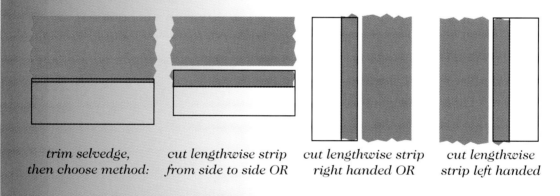

*trim selvedge,
then choose method:*   *cut lengthwise strip
from side to side OR*   *cut lengthwise strip
right handed OR*   *cut lengthwise
strip left handed*

3. Rotary Cutting Patches

While Grandma would probably embrace rotary cutting wholeheartedly, I think she would have some reservations about some of today's shortcuts. I'm not saying we should go back to the old way. I doubt that Grandma, herself, would. Tracing around templates and cutting with scissors were slow and tedious.

I own a good pair of scissors. I use them to cut coupons out of the paper. My scissors haven't touched fabric in years. That's probably true for most of you reading this. Still, Gran had a good thing going. The old way of cutting individual patches was straightforward, accurate, and versatile. You cut the shape you saw. You could count

on it fitting. And you could cut any shape that might come up.

Wouldn't it be wonderful if we could have the best of both worlds? Guess what? We can! We can have the speed of rotary cutting and the straightforward simplicity of cutting patches. We can toss out the tracing and the tedium of the old ways along with the design limitations of the new. All we need to do is to rotary cut patches.

I know it sounds slow, but it's not. Cutting out shapes gets a bad rap simply because it seems a lot like the old way. It's not: You can cut through multiple layers. You don't need templates. You don't need to mark anything. And you can use your trusty rotary cutter instead of scissors.

Hear me out on this. When you cut a finished triangle, you have to make three cuts, one for each side. No shortcut in the world will allow you to make a triangle with fewer than three cuts (although some "shortcuts" require four or five!). Today, many shortcuts have you cutting in stages, sewing units together, and then cutting them down again. You haven't eliminated any steps. You still need three cuts to make a triangle. You have just broken up the cutting with a little sewing.

Imagine how fast the sewing will go when you have finished cutting out the patches before you start stitching!

Here is my best-of-both-worlds rotary cutting method for patches: Layer four fabrics. Cut a single stack of strips first. Leave the strip stack in place on the mat, and pull the remaining fabric an inch or so away from the strip. Next trim the short end at the proper angle for your patches (see pages 16-21). Right handers trim the bottom or left end of the strip. Left handers trim the bottom or right end.

Usually, subcuts are parallel to this squared or angled end cut. Position the rule line listed for your patch over the trimmed end of the strip. Subcut parallel to the end at the listed interval. If you will be making further subcuts, gently slide the strip between cuts to allow space between units.

Continue with the subsequent cuts described for your shape. These cuts may involve cutting the unit in half diagonally or cutting off one or more corners, for example. When you subcut strips into squares or other shapes, keep handling to a minimum. Leave the strip in place and turn the ruler and/or mat as needed. Complete the patch cutting for one strip before going on to the next strip.

While the patches are still in neat stacks of four, trim points according to pattern directions. After the patches are completely cut and trimmed, set them aside and proceed with additional strips and patches from the same fabrics. When you have cut all strips and patches from one stack of fabrics, go on to another stack of fabrics.

Try rotary cutting patches. It's easy. It's versatile. It gives you total freedom in scrap fabric placement. Grandma would approve.

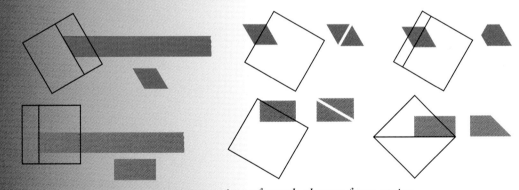

rotary cut a variety of patch shapes from strips

4. Practical Point Trimming

Grandma trimmed her points, but she did it after piecing. Her object was to reduce bulk in seams and minimize show-through. Works for me, but trimming before you sew can do more. Grandma aligned patches by drawing stitching lines. We can align patches by pretrimming points.

I discovered the advantages of point trimming nearly 30 years ago quite by accident. I didn't know a quilt from a parachute.

Someone told me that quilts were made with ¼" seam allowances. Through some perversity of understanding, I trimmed my seam allowances down to ¼" at the points. I thought you were supposed to. My earliest quilts went together easily. Later, when I found out how it was supposed to be done, I was unwilling to go to the trouble of marking stitching lines, but I decided to skip the point trimming. Big mistake! I was making a Lone Star. It was a bear to put together. Without the trims, I had a hard time aligning patches for perfect joints. I went back to doing it my own way.

Trimming the excess from sharp points before sewing yields neater, easier, and more accurate patchwork. Proper trimming of triangles and other shapes having points sharper than 90° not only eliminates bulk in seam allowances and minimizes show-through, but it also helps you align patches perfectly for machine piecing and helps you keep seam allowances even by eliminating dog ears, those distracting triangles of fabric that stick out past the edge of the seam allowances. Even experienced seamstresses often veer off course alongside dog ears, resulting in seam allowances that are too shallow in places, especially at the ends.

Look at the full-size pattern pieces in this book to see how the points should be trimmed. A Point Trimmer tool will help for trimming points of typical triangles, trapezoids, diamonds, and parallelograms having 45° angles.

For other shapes, trace the pattern pieces from the book. Tape these tracings to the unprinted side of your ruler as a rotary trimming guide. The trimmed end of each trimming template should be along the edge of the ruler. Align the cutting line of the traced shape with the fabric patch and trim off the point of the patch even with the edge of the rotary ruler.

trim points with paper template

trimmed points are
easier to align

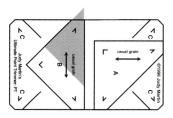

trim points with
Point Trimmer tool

5. Aim for Accuracy

Grandma learned to sew at her mama's knee, but I'm afraid we're not in Kansas anymore. In a quilt class today you are likely to find some who have never sewn. It's hard for teachers to teach to all levels. Some just cover the project at hand and hope the beginners will muddle through. Others, assuming that things aren't going to work out, offer a quick fix. I once overheard a teacher telling her students, "Your sampler blocks will not come out the same size. Some will measure 12¼" and some may be 12⅞". At the next class session we will learn to trim our blocks down and adjust our sashing to fit them all together."

I about had to clamp my hand over my mouth to keep from butting in. The voice in my head was screaming, "Why not teach them how to make the blocks come out the proper size so you won't need to fuss and finagle, recut and resize to fit the parts together?!" I managed to control myself and avoid embarrassing the teacher. However, I vowed I would say something in this book to counter this kind of instruction. The "of course you won't get it right" mentality and the "you can always fix it later" approach do us all a disservice. They are a surefire route to frustration, extra work, and disappointing results. Furthermore, when you have to struggle this way you begin to doubt your capabilities and limit your choices.

My own approach is to aim for accuracy. It is based on my inherent laziness and my total inability to deal with frustration. I don't want to do anything over again. It's way faster and easier to spend a little time mastering accurate cutting and sewing. You can do this in less time than it would take to fix your first quilt, and the skills you learn will save you time and frustration with every quilt you make from here on out. Teach a man to fish...

"Measure twice and cut once," has always been the standard wisdom for anyone constructing anything. So how did we get from there to "Don't worry; we'll fix it later?" Don't you think it's time to get back to what we all know is true?

I have seen people slap that rotary ruler down so fast that I wonder how they could have even found the desired ruling! And I am dead certain they haven't aligned the ruler properly with the fabric. What's the big hurry? Can't they wait to get to the sewing headaches that will inevitably result? You can make up the little extra time it takes to measure carefully when you avoid fussing, finagling, and trimming down blocks later.

Practice holding your ruler firmly in place, walking your hand down the ruler as you cut. Your cutter will be pushing against the ruler, so you need to steady the ruler alongside the blade in order to avoid slippage and crooked cuts.

Cut through no more than four layers for best results. Keep the blade straight up and down, not tilted, in order to ensure that top and bottom layers are the same size.

Most students' accuracy problems are not a matter of cutting, however. It is the seam allowances that most often cause the problems. Make a test block and measure your results to see if your seams are just right. If some patches extend beyond others, your seam allowances are usually to blame.

Most people err on the side of seam allowances that are too deep. If your blocks are not the intended size, look at your individual seam allowances to see where you need to improve. Measure them, if need be.

If it is just a matter of fine tuning, make a block with numerous seams and measure the entire block. Adjustments to any one seam are likely to be barely measurable. A matter of a couple of threads' width can make a difference. If your seam allowance is a mere $\frac{1}{32}$" too deep, your unit will be $\frac{1}{16}$"

too small. If your block has 8 such seams, your block will be $\frac{1}{2}$" too small. A full-size quilt could be as much as 6" too small using this scenario! Houston, I think we have a problem.

Of course, a smaller quilt is only the tip of the iceberg. The bigger problem is the way different parts no longer fit together. Borders don't fit the quilt center, sashes don't fit the blocks, and the large patches don't fit the units made up of smaller patches. It gets irritating to have to fudge and finagle every step of the way.

Learning to get it right from the start is a one-time effort that will pay off with *every* quilt you make. You will need to allow for take up, the fabric needed to go over the hump at a joint. You can do this by letting the fabric extend a thread's width beyond your rule line when you rotary cut the patch. If you prefer, you can make your seam allowances a thread's width narrower when you stitch the seam. Once you find the proper seam allowance, be consistent.

We've all seen quilt tops that ripple rather than lying flat. This can be a result of easing misfit units together. It can also result from bowed seams.

Some sewing machines pull to one side like an under-inflated tire, causing you to veer off course. And some quilters pay less attention to their seam guide in the middle of the seam than they do at the ends. Finally, some quilters get distracted by points extending beyond the edge of the fabric and inadvertently make their seam allowances shallower at the joints. In all of these cases, seams curve rather than proceeding in a straight line, resulting in patchwork that wobbles and bows.

Don't let anyone tell you that you can fix it later. Often you can't, and why should you have to? Take the time to master accurate cutting and sewing now. Getting it right the first time is the ultimate shortcut. It will make all of your patchwork effortless and

inaccuracy leads to bad joints, poor fit

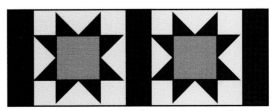

aim for accuracy for perfect results

flawless. You will eliminate frustration and reworking entirely. You will find you can tackle any quilt project and master it easily. Grandma would be proud!

6. Pin Pointers

There's nothing like a new box of pins to make a girl feel special. Wrong! If they're the wrong pins, they can burst your bubble. Here is how I learned that painful lesson: There weren't a dozen pins left in the box I got 30 years ago. At last, I treated myself to a new box of pins. Although I seldom need to restitch a seam because of a poor joint, I soon found myself resewing a simple 9-Patch nine times with unsatisfactory results. (Surely that's not why they call it a Nine-Patch?) I tried sewing over the pins, and I tried pulling the pins out as I reached them, to no avail. When I dug out my old box of pins and tried stitching again, I had immediate success.

My new pins, it turns out, were too thick and too long. They made too much of a hump in the seamline. The best pins for patchwork are very fine (.05mm) and pretty short (1¼" or so). They also have a small head. If you are a careful cutter and sewer and have been disappointed in your joints, try changing to smaller pins. It could make all the difference!

Pinning is essential to sewing success whenever seams are long or have joints to match. I always pin borders, bindings, lining halves, and block rows at every joint and no more than four inches apart. I pin even short seams if they have joints to match. I usually stitch over the pins. Occasionally, I crunch a pin with the needle, in which case I check for burrs and replace the needle if necessary. If you prefer, you can pause to remove the pin when the needle reaches the joint.

We think of pin money as very petty cash. Back in the old days, pins were expensive. Pins were valued, and pin money was not easily come by. Make yourself feel special and get a box of new pins, the right pins, whatever the cost. (You can get a fine box of pins for the price of a fast-food lunch.) Throw out those bent and burred behemoths. Then use your new pins liberally.

7. Finger-Press for Finesse

The word "nail" can mean a lot of different things. There are fingernails, carpenters' nails, coffin nails, and many more. You can nail something shut; in baseball your son the catcher can nail the runner at second base; and in figure skating your daughter can leap high into the air, spin three times, land flawlessly, and nail a triple axel.

Well, you can nail your quilts and score a perfect 10 by carefully attending to the Seven Secrets of Sewing Success. The last of the seven secrets literally involves nailing your quilt, with your thumbnail, that is.

As you sew the patches together for your quilt, crease the seams to one side using your thumbnail rather than using an iron. I lay the unit, right side up, on my thigh. I run my thumbnail along the seam line to train the seam allowance in the right direction. This is called finger-pressing.

You don't want to curve the patch, so run the seamline down the length of your thigh, not around its girth. (Some people prefer a table, but I wouldn't give up my thigh for Cindy Crawford's. Hers wouldn't match my other one, anyway.)

Wooden pressing sticks are available to substitute for your thumbnail, but I prefer to feel the seam and make sure I get the seam line fully open.

Pressing with an iron can stretch bias edges, and it should be avoided until only straight edges remain unstitched. I press my fabric before cutting patches, and I don't press with an iron again until the blocks are complete. Careful finger-pressing won't stretch bias edges. It also prevents unsightly tucks and preserves the ridges of the seam allowances to make perfectly matched joints a breeze.

The crowd roars; you know in your heart that you nailed it; you watch breathlessly as the scores are posted. A perfect quilt! Congratulations!

Part III
Creativity in Action

In this section you will find complete patterns for 27 quilts. These represent color, style, size, quilting, and other variations of 12 designs. Each of the 12 designs opens with musings on the creative process: what I was thinking when I designed the quilts. I go on to discuss creative principles as they apply to the patterns. I give suggestions for further creative exploration and highlight the ideas to be gleaned from each quilt. I show you in glorious color photgraphs just how different a design can look when you exercise your creative options.

Have fun just looking and dreaming. Play at mixing and matching creative elements from the various quilts. Then use the patterns to make the quilts as you see them or as you would like to see them personalized.

I gave you creative food for thought in Part I. You gained confidence from your new skills from Part II. Now, armed with the patterns and variations in Part III, you are ready to flex your creative muscles and spring into action.

For each pattern there are photographs, yardage figures, full-size pattern pieces, rotary cutting directions, piecing diagrams and instructions, and quilting motifs. Whew! That's a mouthful!

Please note that my easy cutting methods may be different from other methods you have used. Be sure to look over my methods for rotary cutting on pages 16–23 before you begin cutting. Note especially the easy way I lay the ruler over the angled end of the strip for some shapes. Note also that, on pages 18 and 23, I offer alternative methods that utilize my specialty rotary cutting tools to save you time and fabric.

What Was I Thinking?

I describe the creative process I went through in designing the various quilts.

Quiltmakers' Style & Color Choices

In this paragraph, I discuss how the makers added their own personal touches to the quilts shown in the book.

Ideas for Taking It Further

Here are suggestions for adding your own creative touches to each pattern, based on ideas from other quilts in the book.

Ideas to be Gleaned from It

These are suggestions for using elements of the designs to add creative touches to other quilts.

Design & Sewing Considerations

This paragraph describes what makes each pattern easy or challenging. It lists techniques you need to know, as well.

Pattern Templates

These are optional full-sized paper templates for you to trace if you use traditional methods. Dashed lines are seam lines; solid lines are cutting lines; arrows indicate straight grain. Some patterns also have quilting motifs indicated with heavier dashed lines. Pink dots are for use in aligning quilting repeats. Points are trimmed for neater, more precise patchwork. Templates for all versions of a design are presented at the beginning of each chapter directly following the "What Was I Thinking?" page.

If you prefer, all of the patterns can be easily rotary cut, following the directions for each individual quilt. Even if you rotary cut, you may find the paper templates handy as a reference for grain lines, letter designations used in the cutting instructions and piecing diagrams, and point trims. If you like, use the templates to check your rotary cutting accuracy.

Photographs

Photos of each quilt show details of fabric, color and quilting. Compare the different versions to see what you like and dislike about them. Feel free to use the color scheme from one and the size from the other, although this may alter yardages.

Captions

The captions identify the quilt's designer and maker(s). In many cases, they identify key fabrics that may still be available. Captions also describe the differences between versions.

Pattern Ratings

Pattern ratings are indicated by spools and lightbulbs beneath the quilt photos. The spools indicate sewing ease and the lightbulbs identify whether or not you need to put your thinking cap on. Use the ratings to help you identify the projects that are right for you.

Spool Ratings

These are quick and easy to sew, with no experience necessary.

Still easy, but they do take more time and have more steps.

These take extra time and effort, but they are worth it.

None of the patterns is especially tricky, but the 3-spool ones include some set-in seams, which I realize some people avoid. (Once you master accuracy in cutting and piecing, set-in seams are no big deal.)

Lightbulb Ratings

Some people think better than they sew, and others sew better than they think. For this reason, my patterns are also rated with lightbulbs. I have no intention of judging your sewing ability or your thinking skills; however, you may want to keep in mind your strengths and preferences when you choose a pattern.

One-bulb patterns are repetitive and can be made with one lobe of your brain tied behind your back. I find them boring. As

Lesley Gore might say, "It's my book, and I'll include what I want to." I didn't include any one-bulb patterns.

These patterns require that you stay awake, but they shouldn't prove too taxing. 2-bulb quilts have two or more kinds of blocks or various ways to turn the blocks. Some 2-bulb quilts are made from rows of half blocks. (I promise not to make you think too hard. The pattern diagrams show you everything you need to do. I subscribe to the theory that a picture is worth a thousand words.) Most of the patterns in this book are 2-bulbers.

These patterns require the full participation of an operational brain. 3-bulb patterns are colored with the overall quilt, rather than the block, in mind. Complete directions and colored diagrams lead you every step of the way. Still, you might actually have to read the directions to make a 3-bulb quilt. If the 3-bulb patterns involve more variables than you feel comfortable juggling right now, you'll be happy to know there are two-bulb versions for those who prefer a traditional look or more obvious construction.

Quilt Specifications

Each pattern lists quilt size, bed size, and requirements for the quilt. Shapes for rotary cutting are listed in cross references, along with page numbers for step-by-step illustrated examples.

Yardage Figures

Each color of fabric is listed in the yardage box to the right of the quilt specifications. Choose yardage or fat quarters. Yardage is listed on the left; the number of fat quarters is listed on the right.

Rotary Cutting Instructions

Each fabric listed in the yardage box is represented by a box colored to match the fabric. The box colors also match the piecing diagrams. For scrap quilts, sometimes many colors are used in the quilt, but only one appears in the box. Pay attention to the quilt photograph to determine what range of colors was used to make the quilt.

Within the cutting box are rotary cutting specifications for each size and shape of patch needed. Shapes are identified by the same letter in the full-size template, the diagrams, and the rotary cutting instructions. Rotary cutting directions call for cutting lengthwise Short Strips of specified widths in the quantities noted. Strips are further subcut into the shapes shown in miniature icons. Dimensions for the subcuts are listed in the box. Until you are familiar with my easy methods, refer to pages 16–23 for step-by-step illustrated directions for cutting each shape.

A Note About Borders

Border dimensions include seam allowances. They do *not* include any extra in case of sewing inaccuracies. (Most people err on the side of making their patchwork too small, anyway.) Add a little extra if it makes you feel better. For quilts with pieced borders and 60° triangles, inner side borders may have different widths from the top/bottom borders. This is needed for fit.

A Note About Bindings

The term "folded binding" denotes binding that is two-layers thick. It is made by folding the strip in half lengthwise, with right sides out; the two raw edges together are stitched to the front of the quilt; then the binding is wrapped around the quilt's edge and the fold is hand stitched on the back.

Piecing Diagrams

Colored piecing diagrams with captions show you each step of making the quilt. A letter is assigned to each patch type. Blocks are exploded to show the first patches joined into sub-units and also to show sub-units joined to make larger units or rows. Generally, the first patches to be joined are close together, and the later parts are farther and farther apart in the diagram.

Quilting Patterns

Most of the quilting patterns here are suitable for machine quilting in a continuous line as well as for hand quilting. Instructions describe unmarked quilting as well as use of specific motifs from the book. Quilting details are diagrammed as needed. Where stippling is called for, it is not shown in the diagrams, but it is mentioned in the text. Some of the designs are used in more than one quilt. The text will indicate where to find the full-size quilting motif in such instances. Feel free to mix and match quilting motifs from various quilts.

Help Boxes

You will find useful information not only in the "Empowering Know-How" section, but also in colored boxes throughout the pattern section. Don't miss these gems.

Patchwork Patterns

Grandmother's Wedding Ring

& Grandmother's Diamond Ring

What Was I Thinking?

The traditional Double Wedding Ring provided the main inspiration for my Grandmother's Wedding Ring. In spite of its tricky curves, Double Wedding Ring is among the favorite quilt patterns of all time. The interlocking circles make a fascinating pattern, and the design is an excellent vehicle for scrap fabrics. In fact, the scrappy quality is a big component of the appeal of Wedding Ring quilts.

Over the years, I have designed numerous patterns that take the best of the Wedding Ring—the illusion of the interlocking rings and the unrestrained use of scrap fabrics—and eliminated the curved piecing. My best known example is probably Tennessee Waltz.

When I designed Grandmother's Wedding Ring, I set out to once again achieve the effect of interlocking rings with scraps. Being a particular fancier of stars, I thought I'd throw a few of those in for good measure. I started with the stars and built the chains out from there. I used hexagonal rings and diamond-shaped intersections to approximate the Wedding Ring pattern without the curves. I added hexagons and stars in a motif reminiscent of a Grandmother's Flower Garden to embellish the rings.

I divided the rings into triangles to show off my scraps. For a simpler variation, I substituted diamonds for the triangles in the Grandmother's Diamond Ring on page 54.

Quiltmakers' Style & Color Choices

Grandmother's Wedding Ring is attractive in any style and color scheme. Jane Bazyn used just 5 current prints in cream, navy, sage, and turkey red for the quilt on page 42. Diane Tomlinson tried an Amish-inspired look using aqua, mauve, and other hand-dyed solids on a solid black background for her version on page 46. I used scraps in contemporary fall-colored fabrics with the background cut from gradated tans for the quilt on page 38. Chris Hulin used cool colored batiks against a pale blue contemporary print for the variation on page 50. Margy Sieck used reproduction '30s prints in assorted pastels on muslin for the Diamond Wedding Ring on page 54.

In Jane's, Diane's, and Margy's versions on pages 42, 46, and 54, units were colored according to an overall, uniform plan. In my version (page 38), triangles in a ring were made from just 2 fabrics. Two different fabrics were used for each ring. In Chris's version (page 50), triangles were colored to form star shapes. These two versions need to be planned on a design wall.

In Margy's version (page 54), colored triangles surround the stars, defining the edges of the hexagons for a different look.

The large open spaces in the hexagons and borders call for elaborate quilting. The various Grandmother's Wedding Ring quilts shown in this book are quilted in four different motifs. Note the use of Carnations, Sprigs, Feathers, and Baptist Fans. The Lotus and Daisy quilting motifs on pages 71 and 174 might also be adapted for use here.

Ideas for Taking Grandmother's Wedding Ring Further

Grandmother's Wedding Ring does not lend itself to major changes in size. Fewer blocks would offer too little repetition to establish a coherent pattern. However, the quilt can be sized for a generous twin to queen/king by adjusting the borders. Borrow the border treatment from the version having your preferred quilt dimensions.

Make Diamond Wedding Ring with a diamond border modeled after that on Horn of Plenty, page 100, for a handsome variation.

Another idea from the Horn of Plenty is to change the colors gradually across the surface of the quilt.

Fancy cut each diamond centered over a print. This will add a lacy look similar to that of Byzantine Flower Garden on page 165.

The Cabin-Cozy Flannel version of the Texas Chain (page 65) offers an interesting idea for the background of Grandmother's Wedding Ring: use a different light background print for each ring.

Ideas to Be Gleaned From Grandmother's Wedding Ring

One of the best ideas from this quilt is to

use a solid background and quilt lavishly.

The wide quilted border edged with a narrow pieced band is another idea that could be used in other quilts.

The version on page 42 features a border idea that could be applied to many quilts: Double the patch size and make a second pieced border modeled after the smaller first.

Cutting & Sewing Considerations

The triangles, hexagons, and 60° diamonds used in this pattern are easy to rotary cut. However, these shapes may be new to you.

This pattern eliminates the curves that can make the traditional Double Wedding Ring a challenge to sew. You'll need to sew joints of six patches. Also, in four of the versions, you will need to sew accurately in order to have crisp points in the triangles. The Grandmother's Diamond Ring (page 54) cuts down significantly on the number of patches and eliminates the more difficult points.

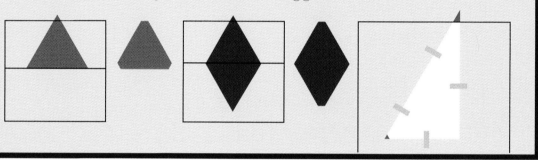

Trimming Points of 60° Patches

For equilateral triangles, cut triangles. Subtract ¼" from the strip width to find the trim measurement. Lay this ruling even with side of patch and trim point. Repeat for each side.

For 60° diamonds, cut diamonds. Subtract ¼" from the strip width to find the trim measurement. Lay this ruling from corner to corner of the diamond. Trim off the point. Repeat at other end.

For other patches, trace the template and tape it to the ruler with the trim line at the ruler's edge to use as a point trimming guide.

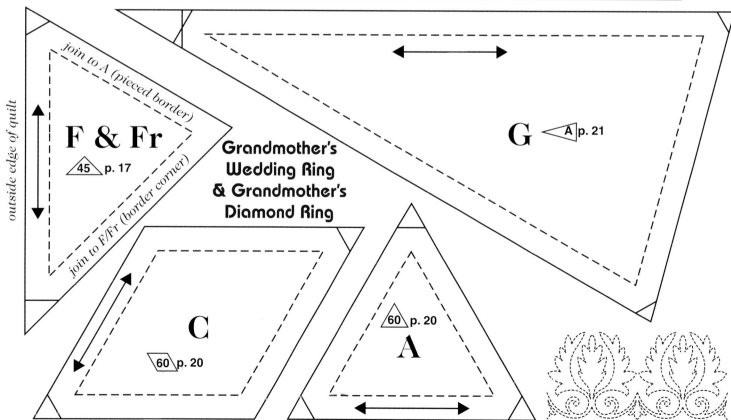

outside edge of quilt

F & Fr △45 p. 17

join to A (pieced border)

join to F/Fr (border corner)

Grandmother's Wedding Ring & Grandmother's Diamond Ring

G ◁A p. 21

C ▱60 p. 20

A △60 p. 20

Sprig border, 2 repeats

E & Er

L p. 16

B

60 p. 20

Grandmother's Wedding Ring
& Grandmother's Diamond Ring

p. 20

D

Grandmother's Wedding Ring
Contemporary Circles

Designed and pieced by Judy Martin; quilted by Jean Nolte, 1999. I chose contemporary prints for my Grandmother's Wedding Ring. I wanted the quilting to show up against the background, but I generally prefer prints for my work. To these ends, I chose a gradated, subtly speckled background print. The gradations permit nuances of color similar to that in a scrap background. In other versions of the Grandmother's Wedding Ring, blocks are interchangeable. Here, a design wall plan is needed to make the two-colored rings. Sewing is just as easy as it is for the following versions, but you need to keep your head screwed on straight to make this one. I modified the sprig quilting motif from the Byzantine Flower Garden border for use in the hexagons and plain borders here. Batting is 100% organic cotton with scrim from Hobbs Bonded Fibers.

Grandmother's Wedding Ring: Contemporary Circles

Quilt Size: 87⅞" x 98¼"
Fits: full/queen bed
Set: 4 x 7
Requires:
28 X, 4 Y, 4 Z
Cross References:
60° diamonds (p. 20)
hexagons (p. 20)
60° triangles (p. 20)
long triangles (p. 16)
45° triangles (p. 17)
design wall plan (p. 6)
sixteenths (p. 23)
reversals (p. 22)
4 set-in seams (p. 145)

Yardage

yds.	or	fat qtrs.
9	background	37
2¼	med. prints	9
2¼	dark prints	9
1	purple prints	4
½	rust prints	2
¾	binding	3
9	lining	36
	92" x 102¼" batting	

Cutting

tan gradated background
borders: (abutted)
2 strips 6½+"* x 85⅜" (top/bottom)
2 strips 6⅞+"* x 83⅝" (sides)

368 A: 60 p. 20
31 strips 2¼" x 18"
60° angle
subcut 2¼" diamonds
cut in half

92 B: 60 p. 20
16 strips 3¾" x 18"
60° angle
subcut 3¾" diamonds
cut in half

92 D: p. 20
46 strips 6½" x 18"
60° angle
subcut 6½" diamonds
subcut 3¼" from diagonal midline
subcut 6½" from edge

12 E: L p. 16
3 strips 4⅛" x 18"
subcut 7⅛+"* rectangles (*halfway between 7⅛" and 7¼")
cut in half diagonally

12 Er: (fabric face down) L p. 16
3 strips 4⅛" x 18"
subcut 7⅛+"* rectangles (*halfway between 7⅛" and 7¼")
cut in half diagonally

medium prints
756 A: 60 p. 20
63 strips 2¼" x 18"
60° angle
subcut 2¼" diamonds
cut in half

4 F: 45 p. 17
1 strip 2⅛+"* x 18" (*halfway between 2⅛" and 2¼")
45° angle
subcut parallelogram 2⅜+"* (*halfway between 2⅜" and 2½")
cut in half diagonally 45 p. 17

4 Fr: (fabric face down)
1 strip 2⅛+"* x 18"
45° angle
subcut parallelogram 2⅜+"*
cut in half diagonally

dark prints
576 A: 60 p. 20
48 strips 2¼" x 18"
60° angle
subcut 2¼" diamonds
cut in half

purple prints
184 C: 60 p. 20
27 strips 2" x 18"
60° angle
subcut 2" diamonds

rust prints
92 C: 60 p. 20
14 strips 2" x 18"
60° angle
subcut 2" diamonds

*halfway between listed number and next higher ⅛"

Construction

Sew 2 background A's to a rust C diamond. Similarly sew 2 background A's to a purple C. Attach these units to opposite ends of a D hexagon as shown. Make 92 unit U's.

Pair each medium fabric with a dark one. Use the pair to make 11–12 each of border units, V's and W's. Repeat for 9 fabric pairs to make a total of 92 V, 92 W, and 102 border units.)

On a design wall, arrange units U, V, and W as shown in the layout diagram below. Start with 6 U's forming a star. Add 6 V's and 6 W's in matching fabrics, arranged in a hexagonal ring around the star. Add a V of another color beside each W and a W beside each V. These are the beginnings of the neighboring rings, which are also made of matched units. Lay out the quilt, referring to quilt diagram to see placement of full and partial rings. Fill in with E's and Er's at top and bottom. Pick up units in order and join them as shown to make 28 X blocks, 4 Y blocks, and 4 Z blocks. Note that you *lay out* the quilt in hexagons, but you *sew* the quilt together in triangular units. Join X, Y, and Z units to make 4 vertical rows. Join rows.

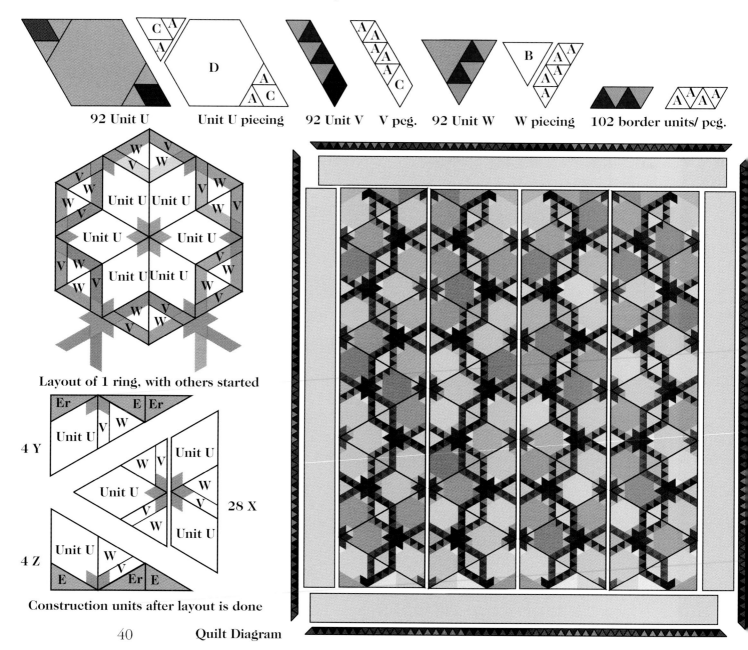

92 Unit U **Unit U piecing** **92 Unit V** **V pcg.** **92 Unit W** **W piecing** **102 border units/ pcg.**

Layout of 1 ring, with others started

4 Y

28 X

4 Z

Construction units after layout is done

40   **Quilt Diagram**

Add short plain borders to sides. Add longer borders to top and bottom. Join 24 border units and a dark A. Add an F to one end and an Fr to the other. Sew to top of quilt. Repeat for bottom. Join 27 border units and a dark A. Add an F to one end and an Fr to the other. Sew to side of quilt. Repeat. Miter corners with set-in seams (page 145).

Mark sprig motifs from page 37 in B, D, E and Er patches. Use the motif in the D hexagon on page 37 to mark the borders, including the pink extensions for the borders only. Quilt as marked. Quilt in the ditch around all diamonds, around border triangles, and between rings and background. Bind to finish. Don't forget to sign your masterpiece!

Quilting   41

Grandmother's Wedding Ring
Simple Wedding

Designed by Judy Martin; made by Jane Bazyn, 1999. The sophisticated, uncluttered style here is Jane's own. Jane used just five fabrics. At center stage is a vintage-look toile. Two contemporary mottled solids, a country-style floral, and a vintage reproduction two-tone print provide the necessary shading and contrasts. Background hexagons are fancy cut to center the floral print. Jane enlarged the quilt by making the cream border wider and adding a border of larger triangles. She then finished it off with the small triangle border used in three of the other versions. Jane intricately machine stippled the background and quilted Baptist Fans in the plain border. The background fabric is from Marsha McCloskey's Staples, courtesy of Fasco.

42

Quilt Size: 95⅝" x 109½"
Fits: queen/king bed
Set: 4 x 7 units
Requires:
28 X, 4 Y, 4 Z units
Cross References:
60° diamonds (p. 20)
hexagons (p. 20)

60° triangles (p. 20)
long triangles (p. 16)
acute triangles (p. 21)
sixteenths (p. 23)
reversals (p. 22)
4 set-in seams (p. 145)
fancy cutting (p. 172)
   (optional)

Yardage		
yds.	or	fat qtrs.
10¾	background	43
1¾	sage print	7
3¼	navy print	13
1	red print	4
½	light red print	2
¾	binding	3
10	lining	36
100" x 114" batting		

Cutting

cream background print
(allow extra for fancy cutting)
borders: (abutted)
2 strips 9⅛+"* x 87⅛" (top/bottom)
   2 strips 7¾+"* x 83⅝" (sides)

368 A: /60\ p. 20
31 strips 2¼" x 18"
60° angle
subcut 2¼" diamonds
cut in half

200 B: /60\ p. 20
34 strips 3¾" x 18"
60° angle
subcut 3¾" diamonds
cut in half

92 D: ⬡ p. 20
46 strips 6½" x 18"
60° angle
subcut 6½" diamonds
subcut 3¼" from diagonal midline
subcut 6½" from edge

12 E: L\ p. 16
3 strips 4⅛" x 18"
subcut 7⅛+"* rectangles (*halfway
   between 7⅛" and 7¼")
cut in half

12 Er: (fabric face down) L\ p. 16
3 strips 4⅛" x 18"
subcut 7⅛+"* rectangles (*halfway
   between 7⅛" and 7¼")
cut in half

sage print
596 A: /60\ p. 20
50 strips 2¼" x 18"
60° angle
subcut 2¼" diamonds
cut in half

navy print
776 A: /60\ p. 20
65 strips 2¼" x 18"
60° angle
subcut 2¼" diamonds
cut in half

112 B: /60\ p. 20
19 strips 3¾" x 18"
60° angle
subcut 3¾" diamonds
cut in half

4 G: <A\ p. 21
2 strips 3¼" x 18"
cut 30° angle (cut off 60°)
subcut 3¼" diamond
cut in half

red print
184 C: \60\ p. 20
31 strips 2" x 18"
60° angle
subcut 2" diamonds

light red print
92 C: \60\ p. 20
16 strips 2" x 18"
60° angle
subcut 2" diamonds

Construction

Make 92 unit 1's and 92 unit 2's as shown. From these plus E's and Er's, make 28 X blocks, 4 Y blocks, and 4 Z blocks. Join blocks to make 4 vertical rows. Join rows.

Add short plain borders to sides. Add longer borders to top and bottom. Join 30 navy B's alternately with 29 cream B's. Join 61 sage A's alternately with 60 navy A's. Sew the two pieced strips together to make a side border. Repeat. Join 26 navy B's alternately with 25 cream B's. Join 53 sage A's alternately with 52 navy A's. Sew the two pieced strips together. Add a G to each end to complete the top border. Repeat for bottom. Attach borders and miter corners (p. 145).

Delete the outer semicircle from the quilt-ing motif on page 118 to use for the fan quilting here. Align the pink center dot with the point of the G patch in the lower left corner and mark the part of the circles that is over the cream background. Mark 7 motifs 6½" apart, stopping just past the center of the bottom border. Mark 7 more motifs starting at the lower right corner and proceeding left. Repeat for the top border. For side borders, mark 7 motifs beyond the corner in each direction. Quilt as marked, quilt in the ditch around diamonds and navy border triangles. Quilt in the ditch between rings and background. Outline the centered, printed motifs in the background, if desired. Stipple quilt the rest of the background. Bind to finish.

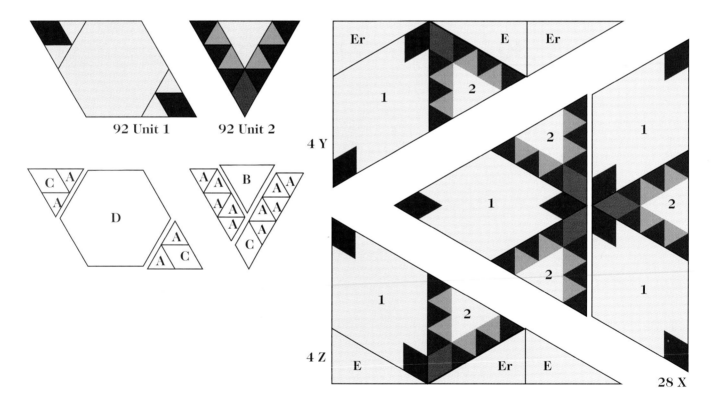

92 Unit 1   92 Unit 2

4 Y

4 Z

28 X

44

Quilt Diagram

Quilting

45

Grandmother's Wedding Ring
Amish Artistry

 Designed by Judy Martin; pieced by Diane Tomlinson; quilted by Jean Nolte, 1999. Diane was inspired by the dark backgrounds, solid scrap fabrics, and abundant quilting of Amish quilts. For a contemporary twist, she chose hand-dyed solids. Whereas Jane used five fabrics in Simple Wedding, Diane used a multitude of scraps sorted into light and medium values on a dark background. Diane's version generally reverses the light and dark usage in Simple Wedding. The use of slightly marbled fabrics and scraps here adds nuances of color. The quilt has a cool serenity thanks to the gentle color scheme and the absence of printed detail. Serpentine feathers embellish the hexagons and plain borders. Small stippling in the background puffs up the feathered motifs. Batting is polyester in charcoal gray by Hobbs.

Grandmother's Wedding Ring: Amish Artistry

Quilt Size: 87⅞" x 98¼"
Fits: full/queen bed
Set: 4 x 7
Requires:
28 X, 4 Y, 4 Z
Cross References:
60° diamonds (p. 20)
hexagons (p. 20)
60° triangles (p. 20)
long triangles (p. 16)
45° triangles (p. 17)
sixteenths (p. 23)
reversals (p. 22)
4 set-in seams (p. 145)

Yardage

yds.	or	fat qtrs.
9	background	37
3½	med. solids	14
1¾	light solids	7
¾	binding	3
9	lining	36
	92" x 102" batting	

Cutting

black background solid
borders: (abutted)
2 strips 6½+"* x 85⅜" (top/b)
2 strips 6⅞+"* x 83⅝" (sides)

368 A: 60 p. 20
31 strips 2¼" x 18"
60° angle
subcut 2¼" diamonds
cut in half

92 B: 60 p. 20
16 strips 3¾" x 18"
60° angle
subcut 3¾" diamonds
cut in half

92 D: p. 20
46 strips 6½" x 18"
60° angle
subcut 6½" diamonds
subcut 3¼" from diagonal midline
subcut 6½" from edge

12 E: L p. 16
3 strips 4⅛" x 18"
subcut 7⅛+"* rectangles (*halfway between 7⅛" and 7¼")
cut in half

12 Er: (fabric face down) L p.
3 strips 4⅛" x 18"
subcut 7⅛+"* rectangles (*halfway between 7⅛" and 7¼")
cut in half

medium solids
756 A: 60 p. 20
63 strips 2¼" x 18"
60° angle
subcut 2¼" diamonds
cut in half

276 C: 60 p. 20
46 strips 2" x 18"
60° angle
subcut 2" diamonds

4 F: 45 p. 17
1 strip 2⅛+"* x 18"
45° angle
subcut parallelogram 2⅜+"*
cut in half diagonally

4 Fr: (fabric face down) 45 p. 17
1 strip 2⅛+"* x 18"
45° angle
subcut parallelogram 2⅜+"*
cut in half diagonally

light solids
576 A: 60 p. 20
48 strips 2¼" x 18"
60° angle
subcut 2¼" diamonds
cut in half

folded binding
24 strips 2" x 18"

lining fabric
3 panels 31" x 102¼"

*halfway between listed number and next higher ⅛"

Make 92 unit 1's and 92 unit 2's as shown. From these, make 28 X blocks, 4 Y blocks, and 4 Z blocks. Join blocks to make vertical rows. Join rows.

Add short plain borders to sides. Add longer borders to top and bottom. Join 55 light A's alternately with 54 medium A's. Add F to one end and Fr to the other to complete a side border. Repeat. Join 49 light A's alternately with 48 medium A's. Add F to one end and Fr to the other to complete top border. Repeat for bottom. Attach borders and miter corners with a set-in seam (page 145).

Mark and quilt the feather quilting motif below in each hexagon. Mark and quilt border feathers (see below). Stipple quilt the rest of the background. Quilt in the ditch around diamonds, border triangles, and between rings and background. Bind to finish. Sign, date, and enjoy your new quilt!

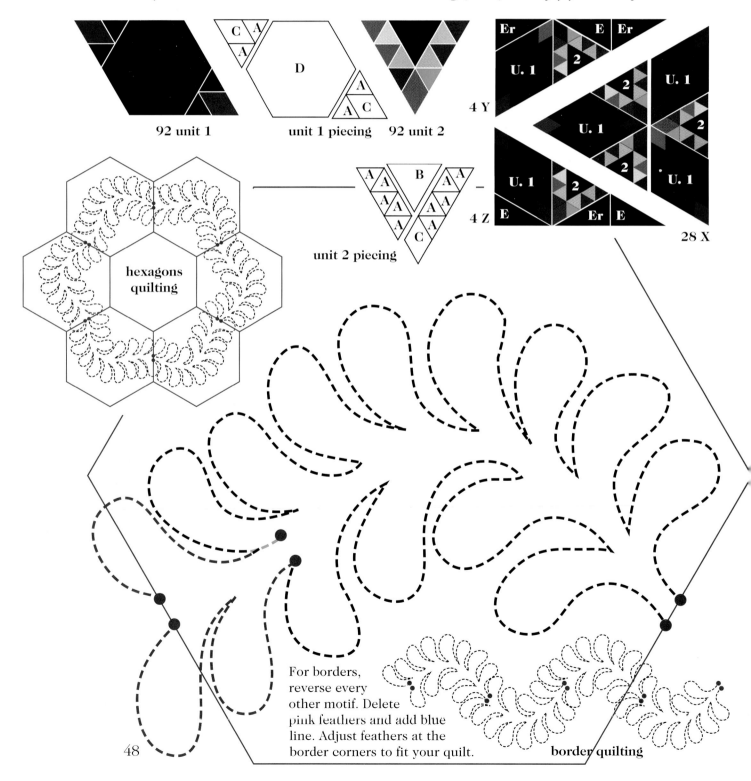

92 unit 1

unit 1 piecing

92 unit 2

4 Y

4 Z

28 X

unit 2 piecing

hexagons quilting

For borders, reverse every other motif. Delete pink feathers and add blue line. Adjust feathers at the border corners to fit your quilt.

border quilting

48

Quilt Diagram

Quilting

49

Grandmother's Wedding Ring
Stunning Stars

Designed by Judy Martin; pieced by Chris Hulin; quilted by Jean Nolte, 1999. Chris made this quilt in her own characteristically contemporary scrap style. She included plenty of batiks among her scraps. Like my own version, this one requires design wall planning. Chris sorted her scraps into medium and dark blue, green, and lilac. Her colors were then arranged to make blue, green, and lilac star-shaped rings. Many Bali Handpaints batik fabrics are courtesy of Hoffman International. Batting is 100% organic cotton with scrim from Hobbs.

Grandmother's Wedding Ring: Stunning Stars

Quilt Size: 81 x 93”
Fits: full/queen bed
Set: 4 x 7
Requires:
14 U
14 V
2 W
2 X
2 Y
2 Z

Cross References:
60° diamonds (p. 20)
hexagons (p. 20)
60° triangles (p. 20)
long triangles (p. 16)
45° triangles (p. 17)
sixteenths (p. 23)
reversals (p. 22)
4 set-in seams (p. 145)

Yardage

yds.	or	fat qtrs.
7½	background	30
¾	med. greens	3
1	dk. greens	4
¾	med. blues	3
1	dk. blues	4
¾	med. lilac	3
1	dk. lilac	4
¾	binding	3
8⅝	lining	36
	85” x 97” batting	

Cutting

light blue background print
borders: (abutted)
2 strips 3½” x 83⅝” (sides)
2 strips 4” x 78⅜+”* (top/bottom)
(*halfway between 78⅜” & 78½”)

368 A: 60 p. 20
31 strips 2¼” x 18”
60° angle
subcut 2¼” diamonds
cut in half

92 B: 60 p. 20
16 strips 3¾” x 18”
60° angle
subcut 3¾” diamonds
cut in half

92 D: p. 20
46 strips 6½” x 18”
60° angle
subcut 6½” diamonds
subcut 3¼” from diagonal midline
subcut 6½” from edge

12 E: L p. 16
3 strips 4⅛” x 18”
subcut 7⅛+”* rectangles (*halfway between 7⅛” and 7¼”)
cut in half

12 Er: (fabric face down) L p. 16
3 strips 4⅛” x 18”
subcut 7⅛+”* rectangles (*halfway between 7⅛” and 7¼”)
cut in half

medium green prints
245 A: 60 p. 20
21 strips 2¼” x 18”
60° angle
subcut 2¼” diamonds
cut in half

dark green prints
185 A: 60 p. 20
16 strips 2¼” x 18”
60° angle
subcut 2¼” diamonds
cut in half

88 C: 60 p. 20
15 strips 2” x 18”
60° angle
subcut 2” diamonds

1 F: 45 p. 17
1 strip 2⅛+”* x 18”
45° angle
subcut parallelogram 2⅜+”*
cut in half diagonally

1 Fr: (fabric face down) 45 p. 17
1 strip 2⅛+”* x 18”
45° angle
subcut parallelogram 2⅜+”*
cut in half diagonally

medium blue prints
245 A: 60 p. 20
21 strips 2¼” x 18”
60° angle
subcut 2¼” diamonds
cut in half

*halfway between listed number and next higher ⅛”

dark blue prints

185 A: △ 60 p. 20
16 strips 2¼" x 18"
60° angle
subcut 2¼" diamonds
cut in half

88 C: ◇ 60 p. 20
15 strips 2" x 18"
60° angle
subcut 2" diamonds

1 F: △ 45 p. 17
1 strip 2⅛+"* x 18"
45° angle
subcut parallelogram 2⅜+"*
cut in half diagonally

1 Fr: (fabric face down)   △ 45 p. 17
Repeat instructions for F, above.

medium lilac prints

256 A: △ 60 p. 20
22 strips 2¼" x 18"
60° angle
subcut 2¼" diamonds
cut in half

dark lilac prints

188 A: △ 60 p. 20
16 strips 2¼" x 18"
60° angle
subcut 2¼" diamonds
cut in half

100 C: ◇ 60 p. 20
15 strips 2" x 18"
60° angle
subcut 2" diamonds

2 F: △ 45 p. 17
1 strip 2⅛+"* x 18"
45° angle
subcut parallelogram 2⅜+"*
cut in half diagonally

1 Fr: (fabric face down)   △ 45 p. 17
Repeat instructions for F, above.

folded binding

23 strips 2" x 18"

lining fabric

3 panels 29" x 97"

*halfway between listed number and next higher ⅛"

Construction

Make units as shown below. Join them, along with E and Er patches to make 14 U, 14 V, 2 W, 2 X, 2 Y, and 2 Z as shown. Join to make vertical rows. Join rows.

Add plain borders to sides then top and bottom. Join 52 medium A's alternately with 51 dark A's. Add F to one end and Fr to the other. Sew to side of quilt. Repeat. Join 45 med. A's alternately with 44 dark A's. Add F to one end and Fr to the other. Sew to top of quilt. Repeat for bottom. Miter corners.

Quilt Carnation motifs (p. 59) in hexagons and half motifs around edges. Quilt in the ditch around border triangles, all diamonds, and between rings and background. Stipple quilt the light borders. Bind to finish.

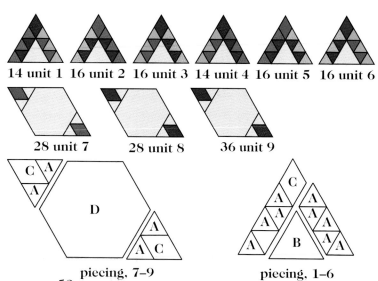

14 unit 1   16 unit 2   16 unit 3   14 unit 4   16 unit 5   16 unit 6

28 unit 7   28 unit 8   36 unit 9

piecing, 7–9   piecing, 1–6

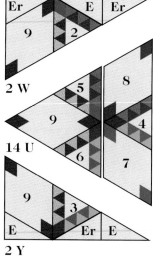

2 W   14 U   2 Y

2 X   14 V   2 Z

Quilt Diagram

Quilting

Grandmother's Diamond Ring
Flirting with the Thirties

 Designed by Judy Martin; pieced by Margy Sieck; quilted by Jean Nolte, 1999. Margy made her quilt in the 1930s style, using reproduction prints on an unbleached muslin solid. The pattern is admirably suited to the '30s style because it combines elements of two of the most popular patterns of the era: Grandmother's Flower Garden and Double Wedding Ring. Margy's quilt is pieced principally of diamonds rather than triangles, and it has a simple wide, contrasting border. Though similar to Grandmother's Wedding Ring, it has approximately 33% fewer pieces, and many joints are eliminated. The solid border and background show off the elaborate floral quilting motif designed by Jean Nolte. Batting is 100% cotton with scrim by Hobbs.

Quilt Size: 84" x 95⅛"
Fits: full/queen bed
Set: 4 x 7 units
Requires:
28 X units
4 Y units
4 Z units

Cross References:
60° diamonds (p. 20)
hexagons (p. 20)
60° triangles (p. 20)
long triangles (p. 16)
sixteenths (p. 23)
reversals (p. 22)

yds.	Yardage or	fat qtrs.
5¼	muslin solid	21
1½	yellow prints	6
3	pastel prints	12
2½	blue border	8
¾	binding	3
8¾	lining	36
	88" x 99" batting	

Cutting

muslin background solid
92 B: △60 p. 20
16 strips 3¾" x 18"
60° angle
subcut 3¾" diamonds
cut in half

92 D: ⬡ p. 20
46 strips 6½" x 18"
60° angle
subcut 6½" diamonds
subcut 3¼" from diagonal midline
subcut 6½" from edge

12 E: ◣ p. 16
3 strips 4⅛" x 18"
subcut 7⅛+"* rectangles (*halfway
  between 7⅛" and 7¼")
cut in half diagonally

12 Er: (fabric face down) ◢ p. 16
3 strips 4⅛" x 18"
subcut 7⅛+"* rectangles (*halfway
  between 7⅛" and 7¼")
cut in half diagonally

yellow prints
184 A: △60 p. 20
16 strips 2¼" x 18"
60° angle
subcut 2¼" diamonds
cut in half

184 C: ◺60 p. 20
31 strips 2" x 18"
60° angle
subcut 2" diamonds

various pastel prints (not yellow)
368 A: △60 p. 20
31 strips 2¼" x 18"
60° angle
subcut 2¼" diamonds
cut in half

460 C: ◺60 p. 20
77 strips 2" x 18"
60° angle
subcut 2" diamonds

blue border solid
border: (abutted)
2 strips 6½" x 84½" (top/bottom)
2 strips 6½" x 83⅝" (sides)

OR 21 strips 6½" x 18"

folded binding
23 strips 2" x 18"

lining fabric
3 panels 30" x 99"

Construction

Make 92 unit 1's and 92 unit 2's as shown. From these, make 28 X blocks, 4 Y blocks, and 4 Z blocks. Join blocks to make 4 vertical rows. Join rows. Add shorter borders to sides. Add longer borders to top and bottom.

Mark the Carnation motif from page 59 in each hexagon and half motifs around edges. Mark the Carnation border motif below in the blue border, rotating every other one. Quilt as marked. Quilt in the ditch around star points and hexagons, and between rings and background. Bind, sign, date, and enjoy!

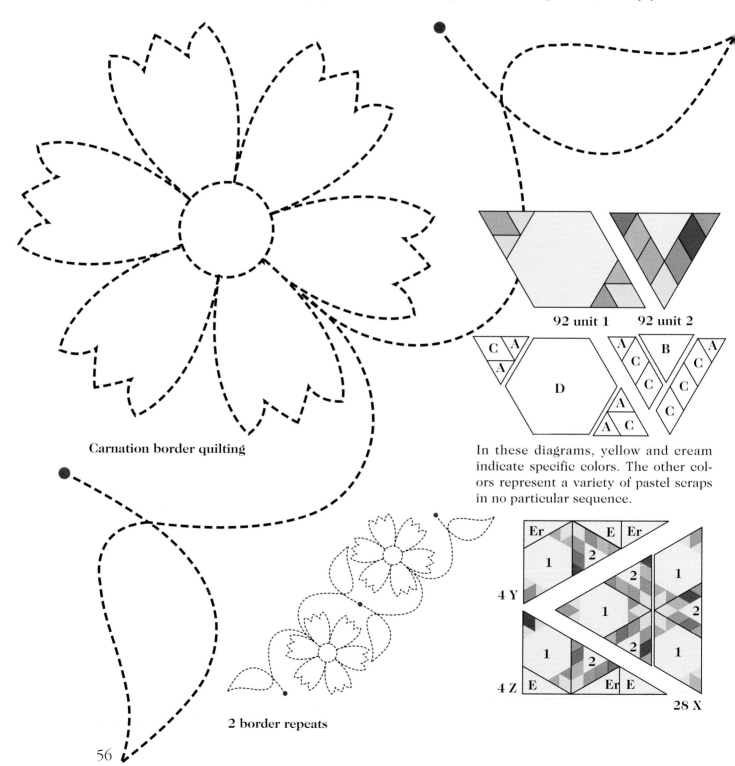

Carnation border quilting

2 border repeats

92 unit 1   **92 unit 2**

In these diagrams, yellow and cream indicate specific colors. The other colors represent a variety of pastel scraps in no particular sequence.

4 Y

4 Z

28 X

56

Quilt Diagram

Quilting

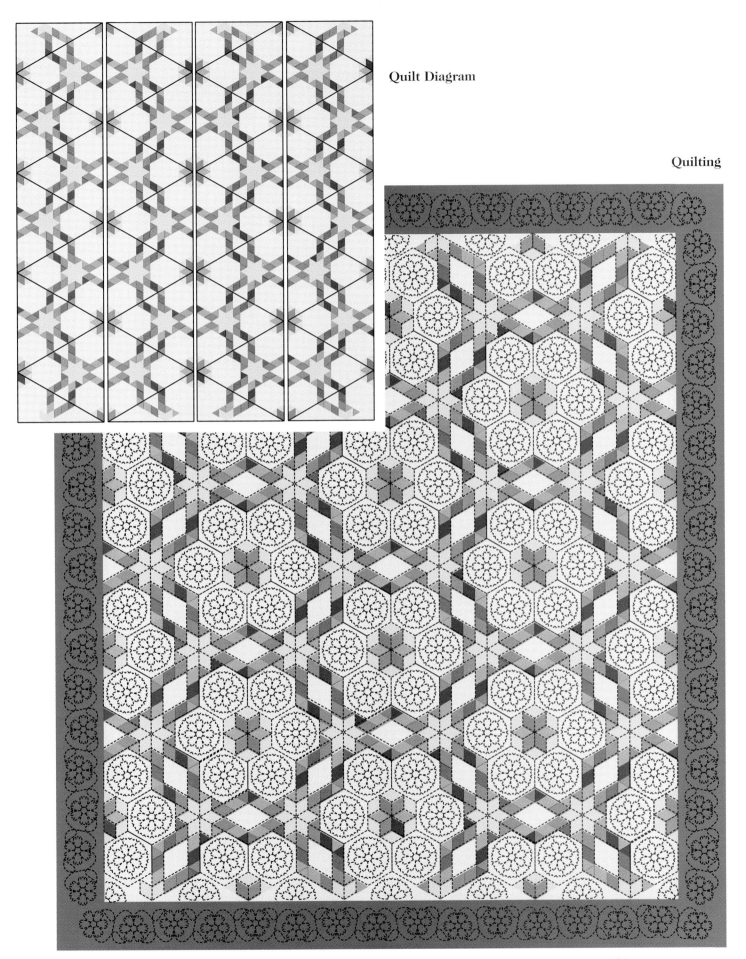

What Was I Thinking?

Texas Chain clearly is rooted in the Irish Chain tradition. Rather than a single chain of squares or a chain flanked on either side by another chain (this triple arrangement being inexplicably called "Double Irish Chain"), I wanted to experiment with two chains instead.

Rather than zeroing in on the chains, I shifted my focus to the background spaces and framed these with rings of squares. To my surprise, the resulting pattern had staggered rings. (Staggering is a design trick I often enjoy using.)

Quiltmakers' Style & Color Choices

See page 69. I first made the Texas Chain quilt from reproduction '30s pastels, including Sweeties from Judie Rothermel and Marcus Brothers Fabrics and One-a-Day Prints from Benartex. The background is unbleached cotton. The multi-colored scheme made it easy to juxtapose fabrics with suitable contrast. (Each chain touches 4 other chains with which it should contrast.) This version requires a design wall or a thinking cap.

My second Texas Chain quilt (page 73) features a background of a Japanese-style print. Squares feature other prints with a Japanese feeling. Mums, leaves, waves, crests, and small geometric line prints, many with gilded touches, are in evidence. I drew the tomato-red, dark blue, light blue, gold, and celery green color scheme from the background print.

The background print is surprisingly busy due to the high contrast of the sweeping ribbons. I found I needed to keep all background patches rotated the same way to minimize the busyness. This is also a version for a design wall.

My friend, Jean Nolte, made her Texas Chain quilt (page 65) out of flannel in country prints and plaids. Another design wall example, her quilt not only has chains placed just so, but each chain is paired with a different background scrap fabric.

The Country Pride version (page 61) is the one to make if you want to waltz through without having to think about what you are doing. It is basically a three-color quilt with dark blue, red, and cream patches in a regular arrangement. Individual scrap fabrics within a color are interchangeable. Karen Cary chose a single printed fabric for the background.

In most of the examples, squares in a ring are cut from the same fabric, with different fabrics for different rings. In Country Pride (page 61), red rings alternate with navy rings. Many scrap fabrics in the same color are used in a single ring in that quilt.

In three of the examples, dark squares were quilted in the ditch. In the Orient Expression version on page 73, dark squares were crossed by an X of quilting. Light areas were quilted more elaborately. Lotus flowers, Carnations, stripes, and concentric circles embellish the various Texas Chain quilts. A small Feathered Circle or Celtic motif would also serve. Remember to use solids or plain looking prints in the background if you plan to quilt an elaborate motif there.

Ideas for Taking Texas Chain Further

The Country Pride version would also look good in a monochromatic scheme having two shades of one color and a contrasting background. This could be done in scraps or in just three fabrics.

This quilt, with its heavy quilting, would be perfect in the Amish style. See the quilt on page 46. Try using bright solid scraps against a black or murky solid background.

You could smatter this quilt with stars, using the 6" star from the border of the Shakespeare in the Park quilt, page 80. It fits perfectly in place of the B square in the center of each ring of squares. Place the stars randomly or regularly for a special touch.

Similarly, you could smatter this quilt with 6" leaves from Judy's Maple Leaf (page 129).

You could borrow the whimsical color scheme and the notion of centering prints in the patches from Byzantine Flower Garden on page 170. Your Texas Chain quilt would take on a new look altogether.

Ideas to be Gleaned From Texas Chain

The Japanese style of the Texas Chain quilt on page 73 would look good in these other quilts, as well: Shakespeare in the Park, Nine-Patch Variation, and Acrobatik.

The idea of using a different scrap print in the background of each ring (as Jean did in her quilt on page 65) could be easily adapted to other quilts. Grandmother's Wedding Ring is a good candidate.

Cutting & Sewing Considerations

The sewing units in this quilt do not correspond to the visual units. In the colorings on pages 65, 69, and 73, this is a project for the design wall or for the quilter who stays focused. The Country Pride version on page 61 is made the easy way, from scraps in two colors against a contrasting background. No design wall is required.

In any version, the cutting and stitching are as easy as it gets. Simply sew squares and rectangles with straight seams.

Texas Chain

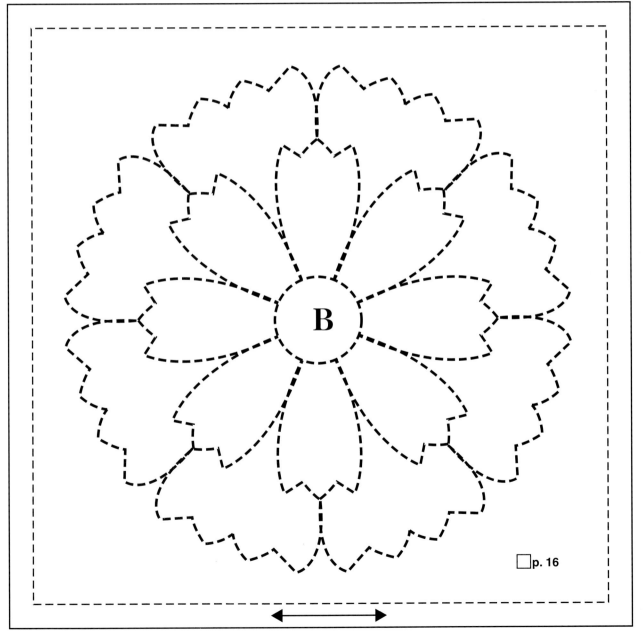

B

p. 16

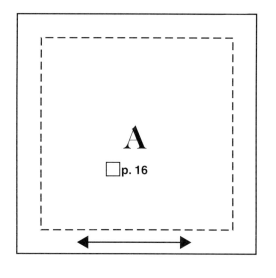

A

□p. 16

Texas Chain

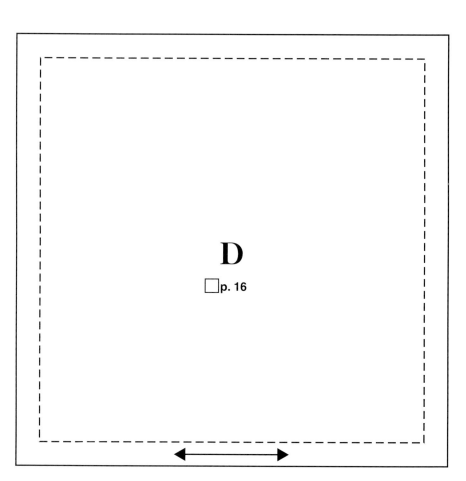

D

□p. 16

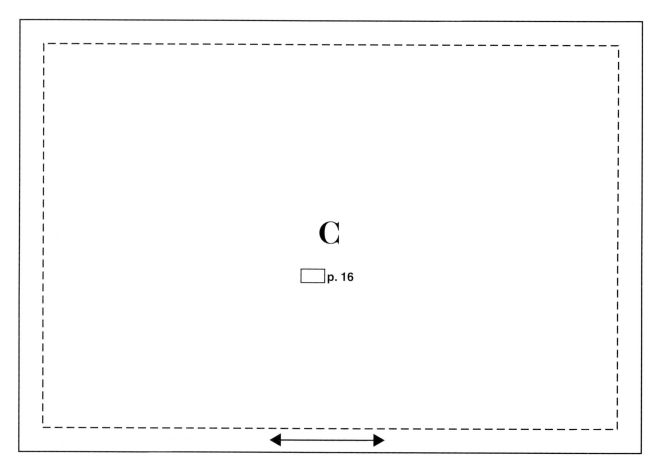

C

□p. 16

Texas Chain
Country Pride

Designed by Judy Martin; pieced by Karen Cary; quilted by Jean Nolte, 1999. This is an easy pattern to sew, and this version is also easy on the noggin. Karen made her country quilt from units of red scraps and blue ones, which she alternated in the quilt. A subtle cream print provides a restful background. Red, cream, and blue squares form a checked border. Quilting is done in the same Carnation pattern used for the Diamond Wedding Ring quilt on page 54. Batting is a cotton blend from Hobbs.

Texas Chain: Country Pride

Quilt Size: 62" x 74"
Fits: wall or throw quilt
Set: 15 rows of 9 units
Requires:
12 R
12 S
16 T
24 U

18 V
33 W
33 X
14 Y
2 Z

Cross References:
squares (p. 16)
rectangles (p. 16)

yds.	Yardage or	fat qtrs.
3	cream print	15
1½	red prints	6
1½	dk. blue prints	6
½	binding	2
4¾	lining	20
	66" x 78" batting	

Cutting

cream print for background
Cut off a piece 45" x 63" from
which to cut:

borders: (abutted)
2 strips 2½" x 62½" (sides)
2 strips 2½" x 54½" (top/bottom)

Cut remainder of this piece of
fabric into 3 lengths of 21"
from which to cut the following:

25 B: ☐ **p. 16**
9 strips 6½" x 21"
subcut 6½" squares

12 C: ☐ **p. 16**
6 strips 4½" x 21"
subcut 6½" rectangles

4 D: ☐ **p. 16**
1 strip 4½" x 21"
subcut 4½" squares

Cut remaining fabric into 2 lengths
of ½ yard from which to cut:

254 A: ☐ **p. 16**
43 strips 2½" x 18"
subcut 2½" squares

red prints
248 A: ☐ **p. 16**
42 strips 2½" x 18"
subcut 2½" squares

dark blue prints
232 A: ☐ **p. 16**
39 strips 2½" x 18"
subcut 2½" squares

folded binding
18 strips 2" x 18"

lining fabric
2 panels 33¼" x 78"

Construction

Make units as shown on page 63. Arrange them as shown on page 64. For rows 1 and 15, join 4 T units alternately with 3 C rectangles; sew a D square to each end. For rows 2, 6, 10, and 14, join 4 B squares alternately with 3 R units; sew a T unit to each end. For rows 3, 5, 7, 9, 11, and 13, sew 4 U units alternately with 3 V units; sew a Y unit to each end. For rows 4, 8, and 12, join 4 S units alternately with 3 B squares; sew a C rectangle to each end. Join rows as shown on page 64. Add plain side borders, then top and bottom borders.

Join 9 W units alternately with 9 X units. Repeat. Sew a Y to the X end of one and a Z to the W end of the other. Sew to sides of quilt as shown on page 64. Sew 8 X units alternately with 7 W units; sew a Y to the X end. Sew to top of quilt. Join 8 W alternately with 7 X; sew a Z to the W end. Attach to bottom of quilt.

Mark and quilt the Carnation motif from page 59 in B patches. Also mark and quilt the Carnation motif in C and D patches, extending into the inner border. Quilt in the ditch around all patches. Bind to finish.

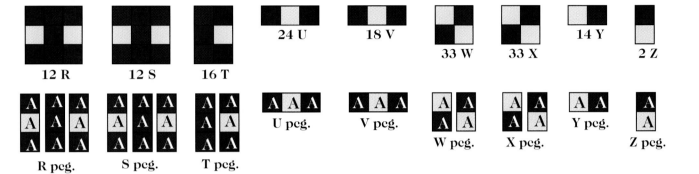

Assembly-Line Strategies for Scrap Quilts

When assembly-line piecing, you repeat a step for the entire quilt before going on to the next step. For example, you might sew all of the A patches to the B patches, then proceed to add a C patch to each of these units. It is important to be consistent when joining patches assembly-line style. Always stitch patches with the same lead edge and the same patch on top. As long as you don't make a mistake and repeat it, assembly-line piecing is unquestionably efficient.

I often adapt assembly-line sewing to make one or two blocks at a time. This works well for scrap quilts or samplers where the fabrics or pattern change for each block. I chain piece four or eight units alike, snip them apart, then go on to the next step. I can chain piece without having to plan or cut far ahead.

Backtack, Don't Backtrack

When I began making quilts, I backtacked to secure the ends of my patchwork seams out of habit. I was thankful for the habit when I had small children who might have unraveled less secure seams. Now that I am having some of my tops quilted on a quilting machine, I am doubly thankful for the habit. My quilter friend, Jean Nolte, tells me that mounting the quilt on a quilting machine stresses the seams, sometimes to the point of popped stitches and unraveled edges. Backtacking, she reports, stands up to the stresses. It can be such a hassle to restitch unraveled seams. Make it a habit to backtack to avoid the headache. You can bactack even if you chain piece. Here's how.

I have found that stitching over the edge of the fabric in reverse can result in tangles. Consequently, I make it a point to start and end each seam with a forward stitch. Start by going forward, then backing up to about one stitch shy of the edge. Then go forward again. At the far end, start reversing when you are one stitch shy of the end. After backtacking a few stitches, proceed forward over the edge and onto the next patch in the chain. Repeat.

Quilt Diagram

Quilting

D	C	C	C	D |#1
B	B	B	B	#2

#3

C B B B C #4

#5

#6

#7

#8

#9

#10

#11

#12

#13

#14

#15

Y

Z

64

Texas Chain
Cabin-Cozy Flannel

Designed by Judy Martin; made by Jean Nolte, 1999. Jean chose country flannels for her version of the Texas Chain. Here, each ring of squares is a different fabric, and the background for each ring also varies. The sewing is a breeze, but you'll need to keep your head screwed on straight. Arranging units on a design wall will help you organize the rows for sewing. Quilting is in a simple pattern of concentric circles. Batting is 100% cotton with scrim from Hobbs.

Texas Chain: Cabin-Cozy Flannel

Quilt Size: 62" x 74"
Fits: throw or wall quilt
Set: 4 x 4 sets
Requires:
25 whole sets

6 half sets
Cross References:
squares (p. 16)
rectangles (p. 16)
design wall plan (p. 6)

Yardage		
yds.	or	fat qtrs.
3¼	buff prints	13
2	border fabric	3
3½	dark/mediums	14
½	binding	2
4¾	lining	20
66" x 78"	batting	

Cutting

buff background prints
You will need totals of 144 A, 25 B, 12 C, & 4 D.

FROM *EACH OF 12* FAT QUARTERS CUT

2 B: ☐ **p. 16**
1 strip 6½" x 18" (x 12 fabrics)
subcut 6½" squares

12 A: ☐ **p. 16**
2 strips 2½" x 18" (x 12 fabrics)
 subcut 2½" squares

1 C, 1D: ☐ **p. 16** ☐ **p. 16**
1 strip 4½" x 18" (x 12 fabrics)
subcut 6½", 4½" (You only need a
   total of 4 D's at 4½".)

From the remaining fat quarter cut:

1 B, 4 A: ☐ **p. 16**
1 strip 6½" x 18"
subcut one 6½" square; cut strip
   down to 2½"; cut four 2½" squares

buff border fabric
borders: (abutted)
2 strips 2½" x 62½" (sides)
2 strips 2½" x 54½" (top/bottom)

dark/medium prints
You will need a total of 574 A.

FROM EACH FAT QUARTER CUT

41 A: ☐ **p. 16**
7 strips 2½" x 18" (x 14 fabrics)
subcut 2½" squares

brown binding fabric
18 strips 2" x 18"

lining fabric
2 panels 33¼" x 78"

Construction

Sew a buff A between 2 matching dark/medium print A's to make unit Y. Repeat to make 4 Y units using the same two prints. Sew two of these units to opposite sides of a matching buff B square to make unit Z. Arrange these on a design wall, along with matching dark/medium A squares to make a whole set, as shown on page 67. *Do not sew the set elements together yet.* Make 21 whole sets and 4 whole sets (left edge).

Make a Y unit, and arrange with C, 2 matching buff A's and 4 or 5 matching dark/medium A's for a half set. Make 3 left and 3 right half sets. On a design wall,

arrange whole and half sets as shown on page 68. Fill in with matching C's and A's at top and bottom and matching D's and A's in corners. Join to make rows. Join rows.

Add long, plain side borders then shorter top and bottom borders. Make 4 strips of 33 A's. Join 2 of these strips for each side border. Make 4 strips of 31 A squares. Join 2 of these for the top border and 2 for the bottom border. Attach side then top/bottom borders.

Mark and quilt the circle motif from page 67 in each B, C, and D patch. Quilt in the ditch between patches, extending lines through the plain border. Bind to finish.

66

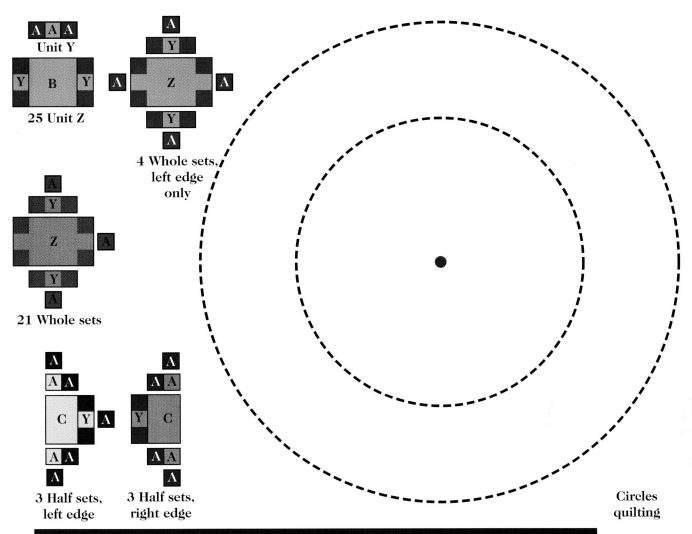

Unit Y

25 Unit Z

4 Whole sets, left edge only

21 Whole sets

3 Half sets, left edge

3 Half sets, right edge

Circles quilting

Chain Piecing Saves Thread, Avoids Tangles

When my friend, Marsha McCloskey, first told me about Chain Piecing many years ago, it sounded nerve wracking. (I pictured myself racing to get the next patches ready while stitching with no hands! It didn't occur to me that I could lift my foot off the pedal and pause to get the patches ready.) Once I tried chain piecing, I was sold on it! No more nasty thread ends and snarly knots, and no more snipping threads on the back of the quilt! You can also save a lot of thread and bobbin winding with chain piecing.

Chain piecing is really very simple. Join two patches in a seam, stitching from edge to edge of the patches. Come to a stop, but leave the presser foot down. Prepare the next pair of patches. Slip the next pair of patches under the tip of the presser foot (without lifting it). Stitch through thin air for a couple of stitches until the second pair of patches

reaches the needle. Stitch the second pair of patches together. The first pair of patches will be attached to the second by a twist of thread. Continue joining patches in pairs. Snip the threads between pairs when you complete a step.

Sometimes it is handy to keep all or some of the units chained together until you are ready to use them again. For example, when I am making a scrap quilt with several patches of the same fabric in one block, I make the units that have matching fabric in succession. Then when I snip the units apart, I leave the matching units chained together until I am ready to use them later. I can easily find the mates when I need them.

Some machines balk at stitching right up to the edge of the fabric. They may push the fabric down the needle hole or make a huge knot on the bobbin side. Chain piecing alleviates this problem.

Quilting

Quilt Diagram

68

Texas Chain
Thrifty Thirties

Designed and pieced by Judy Martin; quilted by Jean Nolte, 1999. Here, each ring of squares is made from a different fabric. The muslin background is uniform throughout. The sewing is a cinch, but you will need to use your head. After making units, arrange them on a design wall. Graceful Lotus Flower quilting accents the plain areas. Fabrics include 1930s reproduction prints from Marcus Brothers and Benartex. Batting is 100% organic cotton from Hobbs.

Quilt Size: 74" x 90"
Fits: twin bed
Set: 5 x 5 sets
Requires:
41 whole sets
8 half sets

Cross References:
squares (p. 16)
rectangles (p. 16)
design wall plan (p. 6)

yds.	Yardage or	fat qtrs.
4⅜	muslin solid	18
5	pastel prints	20
¾	binding	3
5¾	lining	25
	78" x 94" batting	

Cutting

muslin solid
Cut off a piece 80" x 45" and cut:

borders: (abutted)
2 strips 2½" x 78½" (sides)
2 strips 2½" x 66½" (top/bottom)

Cut remainder of this piece of
fabric into 4 pieces 20" long
and cut the following:

41 B: ☐p. 16
14 strips 6½" x 20"
subcut 6½" squares

4 D: ☐p. 16
2 strips 4½" x 20"
subcut 4½" squares

Cut remaining yardage into 4
lengths of ½ yard from which to
cut the following:

16 C: ☐p. 16
8 strips 4½" x 18"
subcut 6½" rectangles

220 A: ☐p. 16
37 strips 2½" x 18"
subcut 2½" squares

pastel prints
You will need a total of 820 A.

FROM EACH FAT QUARTER CUT:

41 A: ☐p. 16
7 strips 2½" x 18" (x 20 fabrics)
subcut 2½" squares

folded binding
21 strips 2" x 18"

lining fabric
2 panels 39¼" x 94"

Construction

Sew a muslin A between 2 matching pastel print A's to make unit Y. Repeat to make 4 Y units using the same pastel print. Sew two of these units to opposite sides of a muslin B square to make unit Z. Arrange these on a design wall, along with matching pastel A squares to make a whole set, as shown on page 71. *Do not sew the set elements together yet.* Make 32 whole sets and 9 whole sets (left edge). Make a Y unit, and arrange with C, 2 muslin A's and 4 matching pastel A's for a half set. Make 8 half sets. On a design wall,

arrange whole and half sets as shown on page 72. Fill in with muslin C's and A's at top and bottom and muslin D's and A's in corners. Join to make wide and narrow rows. Join rows.

Add long, plain side borders then shorter top and bottom borders. Make 4 strips of 41 A's. Join 2 of these strips for each side border. Make 4 strips of 37 A squares. Join 2 of these strips for the top border and 2 for the bottom border. Attach side borders, then attach top and bottom borders.

Mark and quilt the complete Lotus motif below in each B patch. Mark the motif minus one or two of the pink petals, as needed to fit, in the C and D patches. Quilt in the ditch around pastel patches. Bind to finish. Enjoy your new quilt!

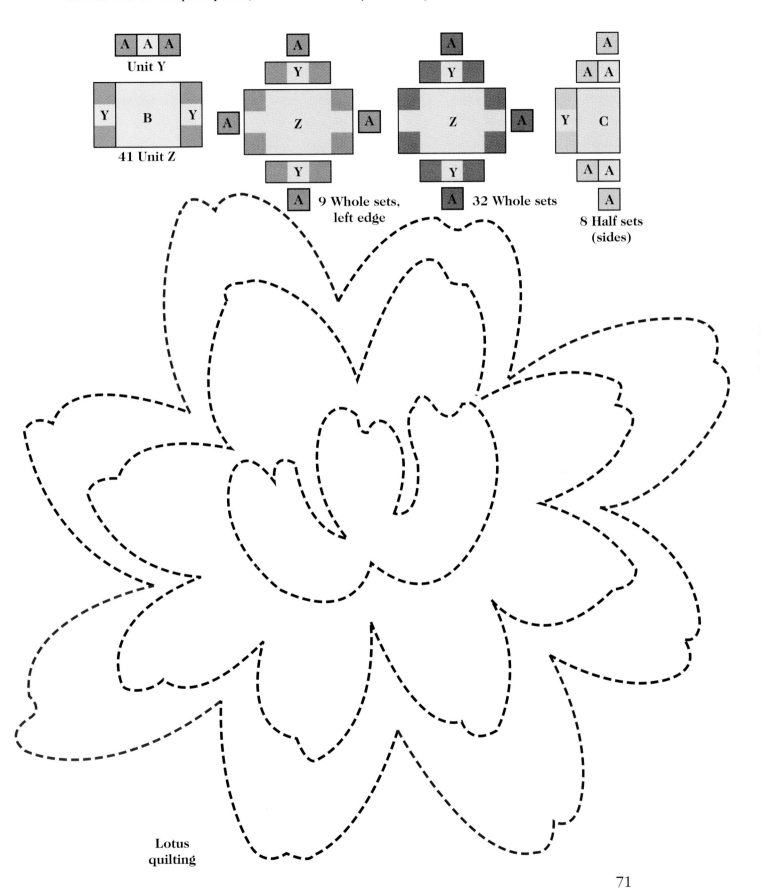

Unit Y

41 Unit Z

9 Whole sets, left edge

32 Whole sets

8 Half sets (sides)

Lotus quilting

71

Quilt Diagram

Quilting

D C C C C D

D C C C C D

Texas Chain
Orient Expression

Designed and pieced by Judy Martin; quilted by Jean Nolte, 1999. In this version, the color placement is the same as that in the 1930s version. However, the color scheme and style are markedly different. I was going for a Japanese look here. The busy background fabric called for a simple, linear quilting plan. Fabric for the background is by Susan Faeder for Balson and Hercules. Batting is 100% organic cotton with scrim from Hobbs.

Texas Chain: Orient Expression

Quilt Size: 86" x 90"
Fits: double/queen bed
Set: 6 x 5 sets
Requires:
50 whole sets
8 half sets

Cross References:
squares (p. 16)
rectangles (p. 16)
design wall plan (p. 6)

yds.	Yardage or	fat qtrs.
5	cream print	20
5¾	dark prints	23
¾	binding	3
8¼	lining	30
	90" x 94" batting	

Cutting

cream print
Cut off a piece 80" x 45" and cut:
borders: (abutted)
4 strips 2½" x 78½"

Cut remainder of this piece of fabric into 4 pieces 20" long and cut the following:

48 B: ☐ p. 16
16 strips 6½" x 20"
subcut 6½" squares

Cut remaining yardage into 5 lengths of ½ yard and cut:

2 B: ☐ p. 16
1 strip 6½" x 18"
subcut 6½" squares

18 C: ☐ p. 16
9 strips 4½" x 18"
subcut 6½" rectangles

4 D: ☐ p. 16
2 strips 4½" x 18"
subcut 4½" squares

262 A: ☐ p. 16
44 strips 2½" x 18"
subcut 2½" squares

various dark prints
You will need a total of 943 A.

FROM EACH FAT QUARTER CUT

41 A: ☐ p. 16
7 strips 2½" x 18" (x 23 fabrics)
subcut 2½" squares

folded binding
23 strips 2" x 18"

lining fabric
3 panels 30½" x 94"

Construction

Sew a cream print A between 2 matching dark print A's to make unit Y. Repeat to make 4 Y units using the same dark print. Sew two of these units to opposite sides of a cream B square to make unit Z. Arrange these on a design wall, along with matching dark print A squares to make a whole set, as shown on page 75. *Do not sew the set elements together yet.* Make 41 whole sets in a variety of dark prints. Also make 9 whole sets for the left edge.

Make a Y unit, and arrange with a cream print C, 2 cream A's and 4 matching dark print A's for a half set. Make 8 half sets in a variety of dark prints. On a design wall, arrange whole and half sets as shown on page 75. Fill in with cream C's and A's at the top and bottom of the quilt and with cream D's and A's in the corners. Join to make wide and narrow rows. Join rows.

Add plain borders to sides, then to top and bottom of quilt. Make 4 strips of 41 A's. Join 2 of these strips for each side border. Make 4 strips of 43 A squares. Join 2 of these strips for the top border and 2 for the bottom border. Attach side borders, then add top and bottom borders.

Mark and quilt parallel vertical lines ½"

74

apart in each B patch. Mark a grid of diagonal lines in the background and plain border, extending from the diagonals of the border squares. Quilt as marked. Quilt diagonally in an "X" through all dark print squares. Bind to finish. Enjoy your new quilt!

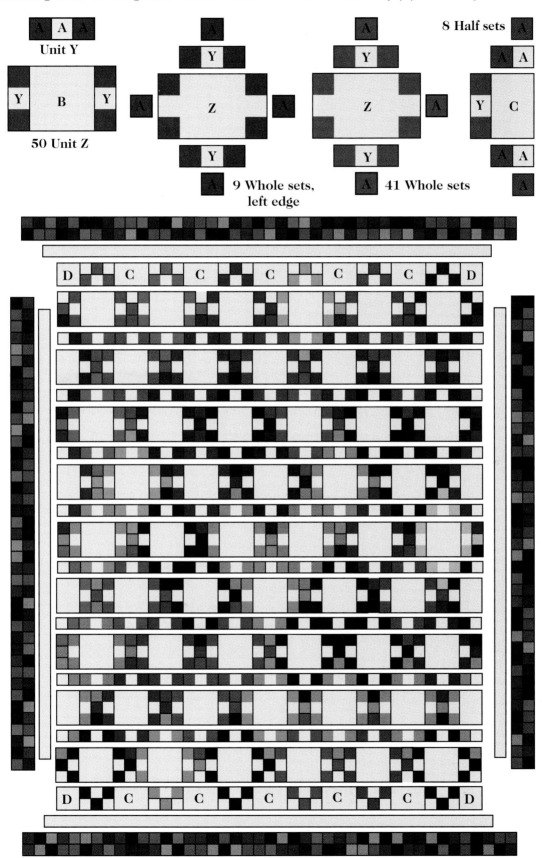

Unit Y

50 Unit Z

9 Whole sets, left edge

41 Whole sets

8 Half sets

Quilt Diagram

75

Quilting

What Was I Thinking?

The traditional Virginia Reel quilt has pieced blocks set alternately with plain squares of light or dark. In my contemplation about possibilities for a Smattering of Stars, it occurred to me that I could superimpose a star on the plain blocks of a Virginia Reel without losing the reel effect.

I have combined Virginia Reel blocks with other blocks before. In *Scrap Quilts* I mixed star and reel elements for Star Reel. In *Yes You Can!* I mixed reels and pinwheels.

I considered substituting a simple Variable Star for the plain block in Shakespeare in the Park, but I thought it would look clunky in the 12" space. A Rising Star would be perfect. It had enough detail for the 12" space, it had a certain simplicity, and it looked good in 2 colors. I used dark stars on light backgrounds and light stars on dark backgrounds. The smaller Variable Stars in the border repeat the Rising Star block centers.

Quiltmakers' Style & Color Choices

Margy Sieck interpreted this pattern in a favorite traditional color scheme of blue and cream. She chose blue scraps ranging from navy to turquoise to country blue. Her creams include white, ivory, khaki, and beige. The far-ranging scraps add nuances that add to the appeal of the quilt. Margy's fabrics are predominantly country in feeling, although she included splashy florals, contemporary prints, and other interesting touches.

Nancy Mahoney made her quilt in four colors: red, cream, black, and gold. Her scraps are more uniform within a color. However, the two additional colors keep things lively. Her choice of prints includes some strong, contemporary pieces as well as a mix of tradional-style prints.

Ideas for Taking
Shakespeare in the Park Further

Make a queen-sized Shakespeare in the Park by adding a row in width to the twin-size version. (Turn the picture sideways to envision the added row of width; the queen-sized quilt's width is the same as the twin quilt's length.) Set the blocks 5 x 5 diagonal-ly for the queen size. You will need 8 V, 8 W, 25 X, 20 Y, and 20 Z blocks and approximately 25% more fat quarters.

Put another 12" block of your choice in place of the Rising Star blocks. Or how about substituting four 6" Maple Leaf units from page 131 for the Rising Star block? Leaves could be turned every which way, and individual leaves could be used in place of the small border stars.

Quilt the edge triangles using the Curlicue motif shown in pink on page 162.

Color each block from two fabrics, and choose a different pair of fabrics for each block.

Shift colors from one end of the quilt to the other as in Horn of Plenty on page 100. In fact, you could use that very color scheme.

You could use just two fabrics if you like. Two solids can capture a popular look from the 1930s. Two prints can have a mid-nineteenth-century look. You can also use scraps on a single background fabric or scraps on scraps. Different looks result when you sort fabrics closely or loosely.

Ideas to be Gleaned From
Shakespeare in the Park

The idea of taking what is basically a 2-color pattern and interpreting it in scraps as Margy did is one you will find useful in many situations.

Nancy Mahoney's idea of interpreting a 2-color pattern in scraps of 4 colors is a creative touch that you could apply to Horn of Plenty, 9-Patch Variation, Judy's Maple Leaf, or Autumn Fantasy.

Shakespeare in the Park combines 2 blocks for the quilt center. This is a time-honored way of breathing new life into old favorites.

This quilt is framed by a border of smaller blocks derived from elements of the 12" blocks. It is an idea that I have found useful. Take a look at the Judy's Fancy quilt on page 143 and the All Star quilt on page 154 for further examples of this idea.

A fun idea that I had never used before this quilt is the color placement in the border stars. Half of them are dark stars on light backgrounds and half are light stars on dark backgrounds. The repetitiveness of the pattern assures continuity in the border, while the color shift provides a little surprise. It also contributes to continuity between the border and the quilt center.

Cutting & Sewing Considerations

Shakespeare in the Park is made from only basic squares and right triangles, with no curves, partial seams, or set-in seams. A beginner could make this quilt; however, she should take care to cut as directed in order to have the straight grain around the edges of the units and blocks.

Beginners may want to read about prewashing, p. 126; chain piecing, p. 67; assembly-line strategies, p. 63; backtacking, p. 63; a bias approach, p. 156; going with the grain, p. 25; and point trimming, p. 27.

Shakespeare in the Park

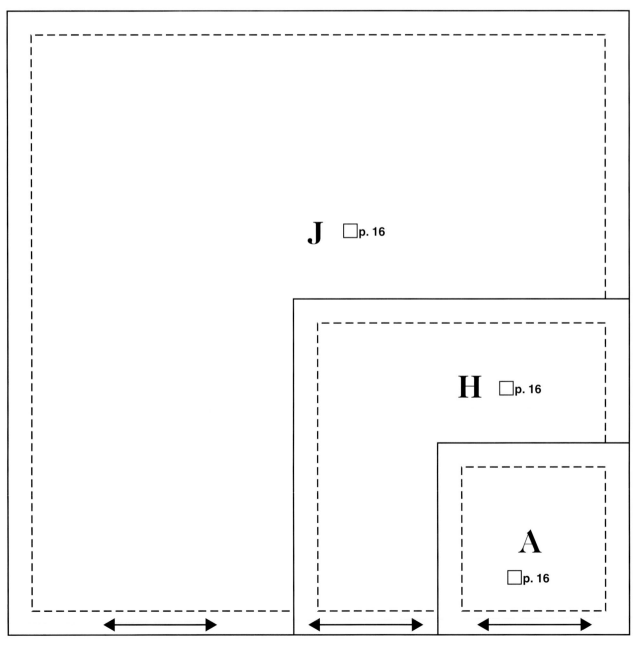

J □ p. 16

H □ p. 16

A

□ p. 16

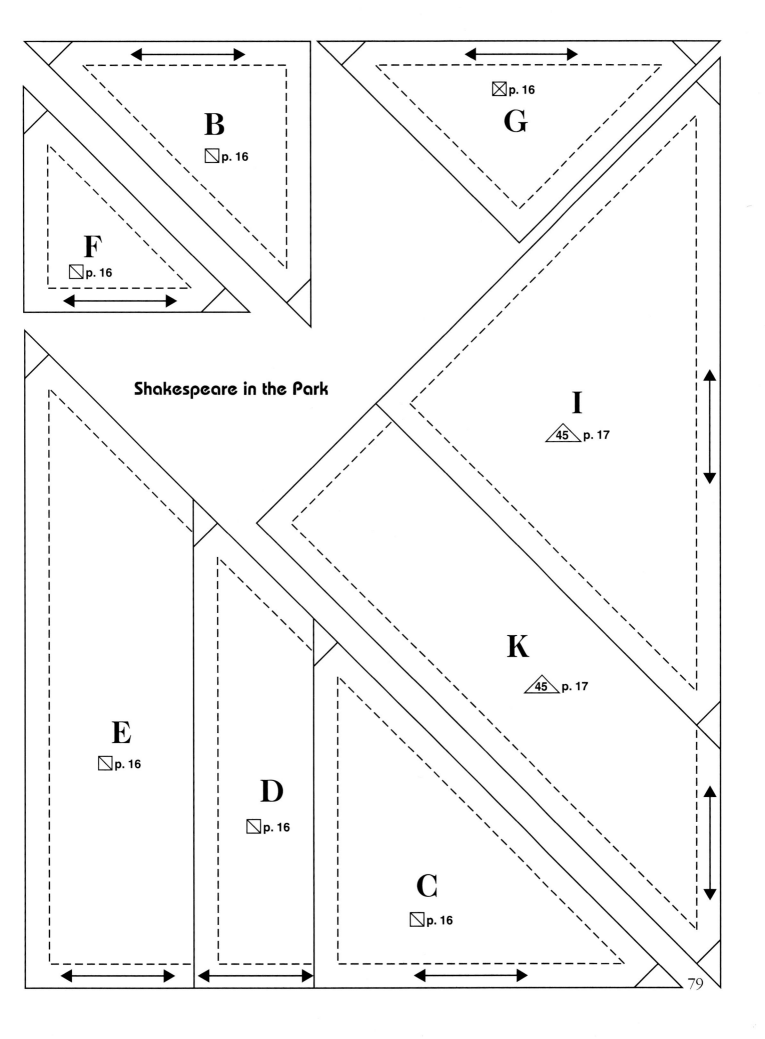

B

⊡p. 16

F

◺p. 16

G

⊠p. 16

I

◁45▷ p. 17

K

◁45▷ p. 17

Shakespeare in the Park

E

◺p. 16

D

◺p. 16

C

◺p. 16

79

Shakespeare in the Park
Country Blues

Designed by Judy Martin; pieced by Margy Sieck; quilted by Jean Nolte, 1999. Margy chose a classic blue-and-cream color scheme and scrappy prints for a country look. Blues range through navy, teal, bright blue and country blue. Lights are also somewhat varied. If you prefer clean-lined simplicity, you can use just two fabrics, perhaps solids. The Virginia Reel blocks are quilted in concentric circles. Smaller circles embellish the star blocks. Batting is low loft polyester from Hobbs.

Quilt Size: 76½" x 93½"
Fits: twin bed
Block Sizes: 12" & 6"
Set: 4 x 5 blocks
   (diagonally)
Requires:
6 V blocks
6 W blocks

20 X blocks
18 Y blocks
18 Z blocks
Cross References:
squares (p. 16)
½ sq. triangles (p. 16)
¼ sq. triangles (p. 16)
45° triangles (p. 17)

Yardage

yds.	or	fat qtrs.
5½	cream prints	22
5½	blue prints	22
1¾	edge triangles	7
¾	binding	3
8¾	lining	30
81" x 98" batting		

Cutting

cream prints
136 A: ☐ **p. 16**
17 strips 2" x 18"
subcut 2" squares

40 B: ◻ **p. 16**
4 strips 3" x 18"
subcut 3" squares
cut in half diagonally

88 C: ◻ **p. 16**
11 strips 3⅞" x 18"
subcut 3⅞" squares
cut in half diagonally

40 D: ◻ **p. 16**
7 strips 5⅛" x 18"
subcut 5⅛" squares
cut in half diagonally

40 E: ◻ **p. 16**
10 strips 6⅛" x 18"
subcut 6⅛" squares
cut in half diagonally

192 F: ◻ **p. 16**
14 strips 2⅜" x 18"
subcut 2⅜" squares
cut in half diagonally

96 G: ⊠ **p. 16**
6 strips 4¼" x 18"
subcut 4¼" squares
cut in half along both diagonals

48 H: ☐ **p. 16**
12 strips 3½" x 18"
subcut 3½" squares

24 I: ◁45 **p. 17**
8 strips 3⅝" x 18"
45° angle
subcut 5⅛" parallelograms
cut in half

7 J: ☐ **p. 16**
4 strips 6½" x 18"
subcut 6½" squares

blue prints
(Cut the same patch
   sizes and quantities as
   listed for cream prints.)

medium blue prints for edge triangles
40 K: ◁45 **p. 17**
20 strips 4⅞" x 18"
45° angle
subcut 6⅞" parallelograms
cut in half

folded binding
22 strips 2" x 18"

lining fabric
3 panels 27½" x 98"

Make blocks V–Z as shown. Arrange blocks according to the quilt diagram. Join blocks to make rows that run diagonally across the quilt. Join rows.

Quilt concentric circles (page 83) in the X blocks. Quilt in the ditch around the stars. Quilt the circle design below in the center of large stars. Quilt a grid of 1½" squares in the large J squares and K edge triangles.

Bind to finish.

6 V blocks

6 W blocks

20 X blocks

18 Y   18 Z

V & W block quilting

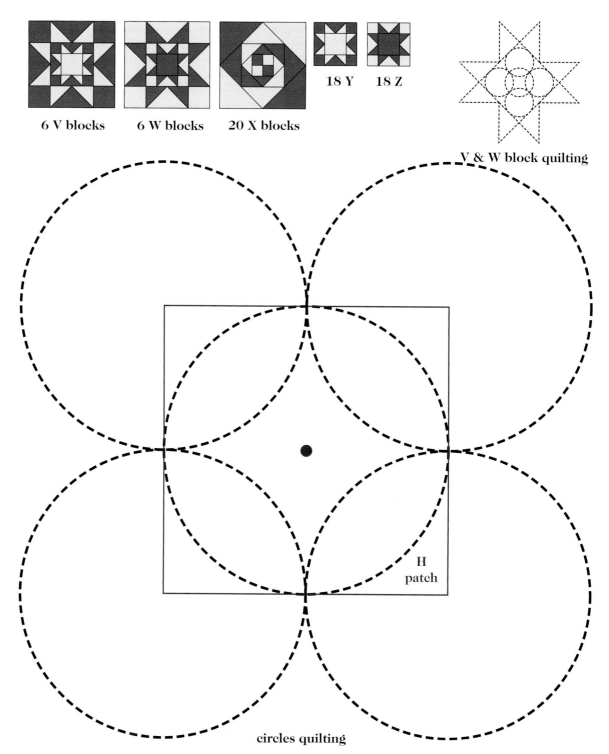

H patch

circles quilting

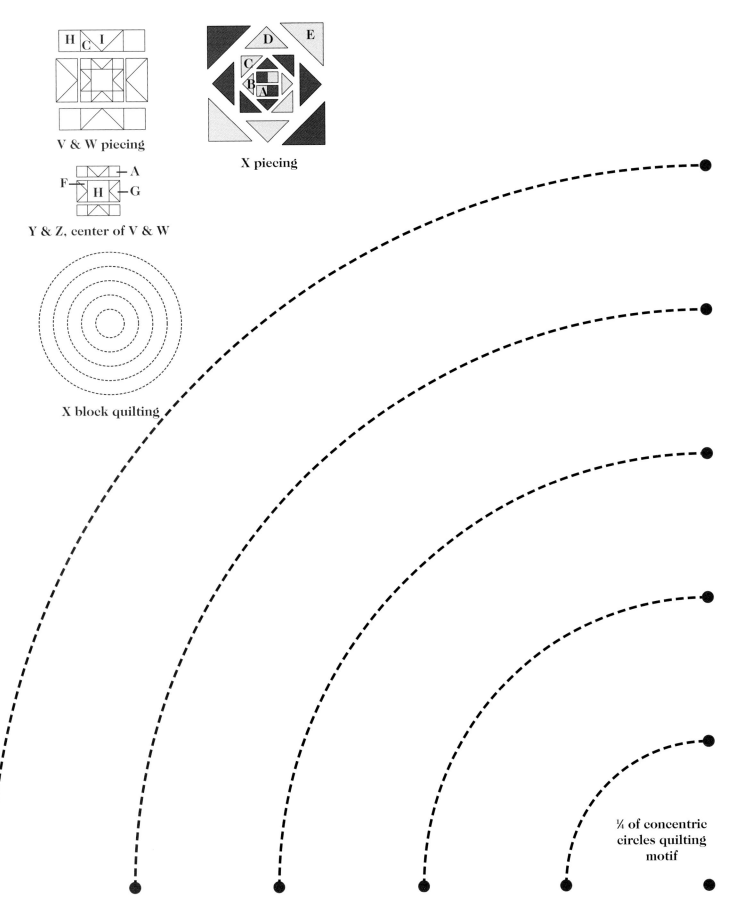

V & W piecing

X piecing

Y & Z, center of V & W

X block quilting

¼ of concentric circles quilting motif

Quilt Diagram

Quilting

84

Shakespeare in the Park
Arresting Reds

Designed by Judy Martin; pieced by Nancy Mahoney; quilted by Barbara Ford, 1999. Nancy stretched the two colors of Margy's quilt into four here. Whereas each block in Margy's quilt is blue and white, Nancy has blocks of black and cream, black and gold, and red and cream. Fabrics are courtesy of Fasco.

Shakespeare in the Park: Arresting Reds

Quilt Size: 59½" x 59½"
Fits: wall or throw
Block Sizes: 12" & 6"
Set: 3 x 3 blocks
  (diagonally)
Requires:
2 V blocks
2 W blocks

9 X blocks
12 Y blocks
12 Z blocks
Cross References:
squares (p. 16)
½ sq. triangles (p. 16)
¼ sq. triangles (p. 16)
45° triangles (p. 17)

yds.	Yardage or	fat qtrs.
2¼	cream prints	9
3	black prints	12
¾	red prints	3
¾	gold prints	3
½	binding	2
3¾	lining	16
	64" x 64" batting	

Cutting

cream prints

74 A: □ p. 16
10 strips 2" x 18"
subcut 2" squares

18 B: ◸ p. 16
2 strips 3" x 18"
subcut 3" squares
cut in half diagonally

18 C: ◸ p. 16
3 strips 3⅞" x 18"
subcut 3⅞" squares
cut in half diagonally

18 D: ◸ p. 16
3 strips 5⅛" x 18"
subcut 5⅛" squares
cut in half diagonally

18 E: ◸ p. 16
5 strips 6⅞" x 18"
subcut 6⅞" squares
cut in half diagonally

56 G: ⊠ p. 16
4 strips 4¼" x 18"
subcut 4¼" squares
cut in half along both diagonals

8 H: □ p. 16
2 strips 3½" x 18"
subcut 3½" squares

8 I: 45 p. 17
3 strips 3⅝" x 18"
45° angle
subcut 5⅛" parallelograms
cut in half

4 J: □ p. 16
2 strips 6½" x 18"
subcut 6½" squares

black prints

(Cut the same patch sizes and quantities as listed for cream prints.) Also cut:

28 K: 45 p. 17
14 strips 4⅞" x 18"
45° angle
subcut 6⅞" parallelograms
cut in half

red prints

16 C: ◸ p. 16
2 strips 3⅞" x 18"
subcut 3⅞" squares
cut in half diagonally

112 F: ◸ p. 16
8 strips 2⅜" x 18"
subcut 2⅜" squares
cut in half diagonally

14 H: □ p. 16
4 strips 3½" x 18"
subcut 3½" squares

gold prints

(Cut the same patch sizes and quantities as listed for red prints.)

folded binding

16 strips 2" x 18"

lining fabric

2 panels 32" x 63½"

Construction

Make blocks V–Z as shown. Arrange blocks according to the quilt diagram. Join blocks to make rows that run diagonally across the quilt. Join rows.

Quilt the concentric circles from page 83 in the X blocks. Quilt in the ditch around the stars. Quilt the circle design from page 82 in the center of large stars. Quilt a grid of 1½" squares in J squares and K edge triangles.

Bind to finish.

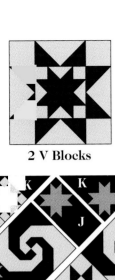

2 V Blocks

2 W Blocks

9 X Blocks

12 Y

12 Z

Y, Z piecing,
center of V
& W piecing

Quilt Diagram

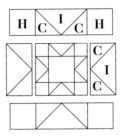

V & W piecing

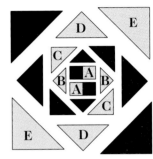

X piecing

Quilting

87

Acrobatik

What Was I Thinking?

Acrobatik was inspired by Whirling Hexagon, a traditional hexagon-shaped block of 6-spoked pinwheels. I liked the look of the traditional patterns, but the 60° trapezoid shape is inefficient to rotary cut. I played with 60° pinwheels made from 60° parallelograms, which are easier to cut. I liked the look, but I had to play around with spacing and construction units awhile before I arrived at this design.

Quiltmakers' Style & Color Choices

Two-toned pinwheels of three different colors contrast with a uniform background in my version on page 90. I used just 7 fabrics: a lighter and darker version of each pinwheel fabric plus the single background. It is made from Hoffman Bali Handpaints, Benartex Impressions Fossil Fern, and other glowing prints.

Jo Moore chose a primitive, country style. Random scraps contrast with a strong gold background from the Everlasting Print line by Brannock and Patek from Moda. This simpler color plan pairs well with a wide range of scrap colors that add interesting nuances.

Ideas for Taking Acrobatik Further

To make a queen-sized Acrobatik quilt, make 8 vertical rows of 15 units each. You will need 48 additional units. Make top and bottom borders like the side borders for the twin-sized version. Make each side border from 16 W, 1 Y, and 16 X. Change widths and lengths of plain borders to fit.

The 7 colors of scraps in Grandmother's Wedding Ring (page 50) could be substituted for the 7 prints in the Batik Beauty coloring.

The blue-and-cream scrap plan of Shakespeare in the Park (page 80) would be an attractive alternative to the warm colors of the Simply Scrappy Acrobatik.

Other suitable color schemes for Simply Scrappy include any of the Texas Chain quilts, the Wilderness Log Cabins, or the Byzantine Flower Gardens.

For a different look, each pinwheel could be made from a different fabric or a different pair of fabrics. This would call for careful design wall planning.

Pinwheels could be made from scraps in three colors. This would be a hybrid between the two versions shown.

'30s pastels and muslin would look terrific in the Simply Scrappy version.

The quilt could be made to shift colors throughout the rainbow or to change from light to dark shades progressively as in the Horn of Plenty quilt on page 100.

You could vary this quilt by changing the pieced border. The Grandmother's Wedding Ring borders on pages 38, 42, 46, and 50 or the Horn of Plenty borders on pages 100 and 104 could be easily adapted, using the patches from the Acrobatik quilt center.

The Daisy quilting pattern from page 174 would look attractive in place of the fern motif in the pinwheel centers.

Individual parallelograms could be fancy cut (page 172) for a stack and whack effect. This would entail the use of a design wall.

Ideas to Be Gleaned From Acrobatik

Two close shades lend dimensionality to the Batik Beauty pattern and help your eye connect patches into distinct pinwheels.

Just a few fabrics can be used to interpret any of the patterns in this book. You'll get the clean lines you see in the Acrobatik on page 90 and streamline the cutting process.

Cutting & Sewing Considerations

This quilt is not made from square blocks. Instead, triangular units are sewn head to foot to make rows.

After joining parallelogram-triangle units, you will need to sew the first unit to the central background triangle with a partial seam. That is, sew it only halfway down the seam line. Add the other two parallelogram-triangle units before completing the partial seam.

In Batik Beauty, the colors go clockwise in one unit and counterclockwise in the other. Turn units so that medium purple touches dark purple, medium khaki touches dark khaki, and medium lilac touches dark lilac.

The Simply Scrappy version has only one kind of unit. It is randomly colored and can be turned any way at all.

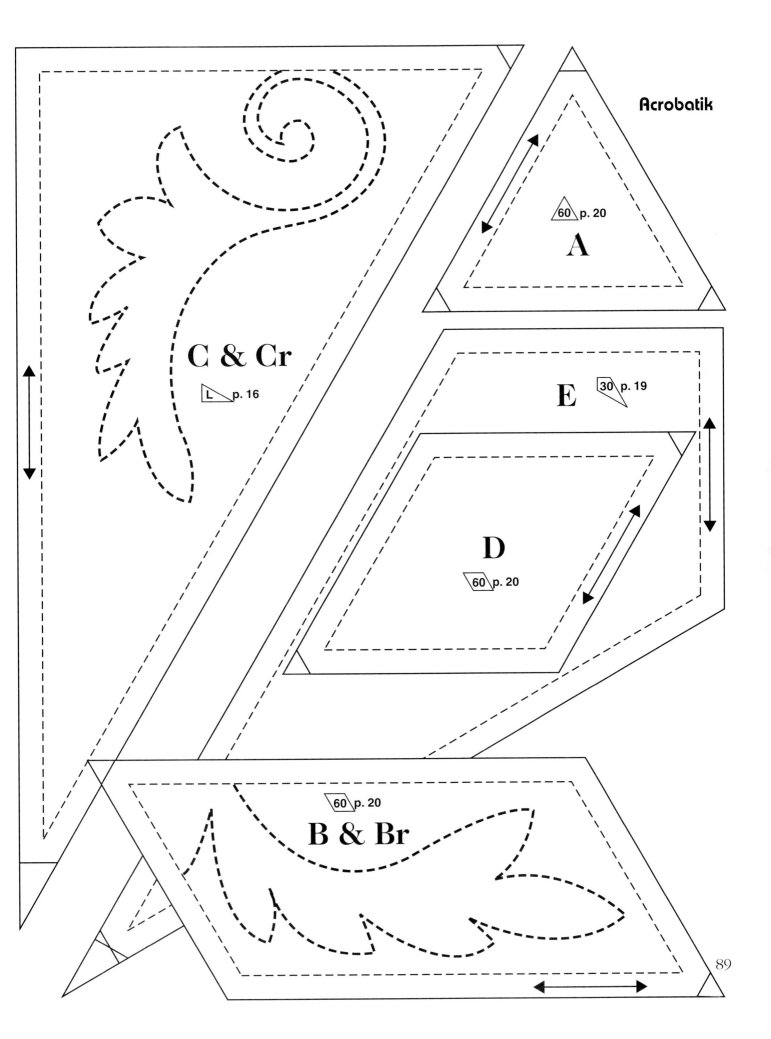

Acrobatik

A
60 p. 20

C & Cr
L p. 16

E
30 p. 19

D
60 p. 20

B & Br
60 p. 20

89

Acrobatik
Batik Beauty

Designed and pieced by Judy Martin; quilted by Jean Nolte, 1999. Seven contemporary prints, including several batiks, give this quilt a decidedly non-traditional look. Two shades each of lilac, purple, and khaki add dimensionality. Pinwheels are quilted with slender ferns. You may find it helpful to lay out this quilt on a design wall before joining the triangular blocks into rows. Fabrics include some from Hoffman, Benartex, and Moda. Batting is 100% organic cotton from Hobbs.

Quilt Size: 66½" x 85"
Fits: twin bed
Set: 8 x 9 units
Requires:
36 U units
36 V units
48 W border units
48 X border units
2 Y border units
2 Z border units

Cross References:
60° parallelograms
  (p. 20)
60° diamonds (p. 20)
60° triangles (p. 20)
30° kites (p. 19)
long triangles (p. 16)
4 set-in seams (p. 145)
partial seams (p. 93)
sixteenths (p. 23)
reversals (p. 22)

Yardage		
yds.	or	fat qtrs.
3½	cream print	14
1¼	dk. purple	5
1¼	med. purple	5
1¼	dk. lilac	5
1¼	med. lilac	5
1¼	dk. khaki	5
1¼	med. khaki	5
¾	binding	3
5¼	lining	25
	71" x 89" batting	

Cutting

cream print for background
border: (abutted)
2 strips 1⅝" x 64½" (sides)
2 strips 2" x 49" (top/bottom)

Cut remainder of this fabric into 7
  lengths of ½ yard and cut:

500 A: △ 60 p. 20
56 strips 2¾" x 18"
60° angle
subcut 2¾" diamonds
cut in half

8 C: L⟍ p. 16
4 strips 5¼+"* x 18" (*halfway
  between 5¼" and 5⅜")
subcut rectangles 9⅛+"* (*halfway
  between 9⅛" and 9¼")
cut in half

8 Cr (fabric face down): L⟍ p. 16
4 strips 5¼+"* x 18"(*halfway
  between 5¼" and 5⅜")
subcut rectangles 9⅛+"* (*halfway
  between 9⅛" and 9¼")
cut in half

dark purple print
44 B: ⟍60⟍ p. 20
22 strips 2½" x 18"
60° angle
subcut 4½" parallelograms

8 Br (fabric face down): ⟍60⟍ p. 20
4 strips 2½" x 18"
60° angle
subcut 4½" parallelograms

border: (abutted)
3 strips 3½" x 18"

medium purple print
42 B: ⟍60⟍ p. 20
21 strips 2½" x 18"
60° angle
subcut 4½" parallelograms

6 Br (fabric face down): ⟍60⟍ p. 20
3 strips 2½" x 18"
60° angle
subcut 4½" parallelograms

2 D: ⟍60⟍ p. 20
1 strip 2½" x 18"
60° angle
subcut 2½" diamonds

4 E: ⟍30⟍ p. 19
2 strips 6⅞+"* (*halfway
  between 6⅞" and 7")
subcut 6⅞+"* squares
60° angle from corner
trim off 2nd corner to match 1st

border: (abutted)
3 strips 3½" x 18"

dark lilac print
44 B: 60 p. 20
22 strips 2½" x 18"
60° angle
subcut 4½" parallelograms

8 Br (fabric face down): 60 p. 20
4 strips 2½" x 18"
60° angle
subcut 4½" parallelograms

2 D: 60 p. 20
1 strip 2½" x 18"
60° angle
subcut 2½" diamonds

border: (abutted)
3 strips 3½" x 18"

medium lilac print
46 B: 60 p. 20
23 strips 2½" x 18"
60° angle
subcut 4½" parallelograms

10 Br (fabric face down): 60 p. 20
5 strips 2½" x 18"
60° angle
subcut 4½" parallelograms

border: (abutted)
3 strips 3½" x 18"

dark khaki print
46 B: 60 p. 20
23 strips 2½" x 18"
60° angle
subcut 4½" parallelograms

10 Br (fabric face down): 60 p. 20
5 strips 2½" x 18"
60° angle
subcut 4½" parallelograms

border: (abutted)
3 strips 3½" x 18"

medium khaki print
46 B: 60 p. 20
23 strips 2½" x 18"
60° angle
subcut 4½" parallelograms

10 Br (fabric face down): 60 p. 20
5 strips 2½" x 18"
60° angle
subcut 4½" parallelograms

border: (abutted)
3 strips 3½" x 18"

folded binding
20 strips 2" x 18"

lining fabric
2 panels 35½" x 89"

Fern Border Quilting
Trace this end to complete
motif at opposite end.

Partial seams are indicated by dashed lines in this help box. This is an easy alternative to set-ins for some blocks. Stitch halfway down the seam joining the first unit to the center triangle (sew to the pink dot). Leave the dashed end unsewn until later. After adding the other units, complete the partial seam.

Construction

Make 36 U units and 36 V units as shown, attaching the center triangle of each block using a partial seam (see above).

Make 4 rows of 5 U units alternated with 4 V units, as shown on page 94. Make 4 rows of 5 V units alternated with 4 U units, as shown. Add a C to one end of each row and a Cr to the other end. Join rows, alternating types, as shown in the diagram.

Attach longer cream border strips to sides of quilt center. Add shorter cream border strips to top and bottom. Make border units: 48 W, 48 X, 2 Y, and 2 Z as shown. Join 10 W, 1 Y, and 10 X; add an E patch to each end. Sew to bottom of quilt. Repeat for top. Join 14 W, 1 Z, and 14 X. Sew to side of quilt. Repeat for other side. Miter border corners (page 145).

Mark the fern motifs from page 89 in B, C, and Cr patches in the quilt center. Mark the fern motif from page 92 in the outer border, adjusting it as needed to fit. (Trace the left half to complete the part of the motif obscured by the book's binding.) Quilt as marked. Quilt in the ditch around outside of pinwheels. Quilt in the ditch around border B and Br parallelograms, extending lines from their long sides through the inner borders. Quilt in the ditch between quilt center and inner border and between pieced border and outer border. Bind to finish.

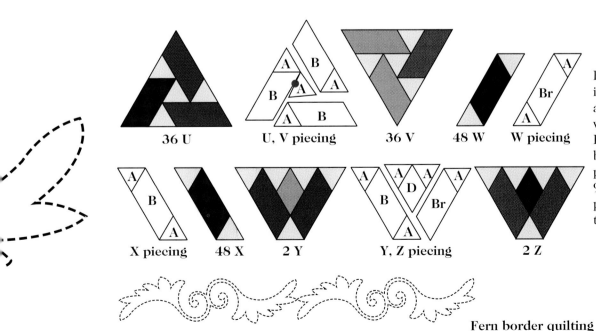

36 U   U, V piecing   36 V   48 W   W piecing

X piecing   48 X   2 Y   Y, Z piecing   2 Z

B and Br patches in W and X units are made from a variety of colors. I arranged the border colors in a pattern (see page 94), but you may prefer to arrange them randomly.

Fern border quilting

Quilt Diagram

Quilting

94

Acrobatik
Simply Scrappy

Designed by Judy Martin; made by Jo Moore, 1999. Jo works in primitive and country styles, and her fabric choices here reflect that. Scrap colors are deep and rich to contrast with the strong gold background. Scraps are placed randomly in blocks, and blocks are all interchangeable. Whereas the Batik Beauty example requires two different block colorings, this quilt requires just one. Background fabric is a striking and bold Everlasting Print by Brannock and Patek from Moda.

Acrobatik: Simply Scrappy

Quilt Size: 52⅝" x 66½"
Fits: throw or wall quilt
Set: 4 x 9 units
Requires:
36 W, 34 X, 34 Y, 4 Z
Cross References:
60° parallelograms (p. 20)
60° diamonds (p. 20)
60° triangles (p. 20)
30° kites (p. 19)
long triangles (p. 16)
4 set-in seams (p. 145)
partial seams (p. 93)
sixteenths (p. 23)
reversals (p. 22)

Yardage

yds.	or	fat qtrs.
2	gold print	8
3½	dark prints	14
1⅞	red border	3
½	binding	2
4⅛	lining	16

56⅝" x 70½" batting

Cutting

gold print for background
border: (abutted)
2 strips 1⅝" x 35⅛" (top/bottom)
2 strips 1¾+"* x 46⅝+"* (sides)
(*halfway between ⅛" rule lines)

Cut remainder of this fabric into 4 lengths of ½ yd. from which to cut:

300 A: 60 p. 20
34 strips 2¾" x 18"
60° angle
subcut 2¾" diamonds
cut in half

4 C: L p. 16
2 strips 5¼+"* x 18" (*halfway between 5¼" and 5⅜")
subcut 9⅛+"* rectangles (*halfway between 9⅛" and 9¼")
cut in half

4 Cr (fabric face down): L p. 16
2 strips 5¼+"* x 18" (*see C)
subcut 9⅛+"* rectangles (*see C)
cut in half

dark prints for pinwheels
146 B: 60 p. 20
73 strips 2½" x 18"
60° angle
subcut 4½" parallelograms

38 Br (fabric face down): 60 p. 20
19 strips 2½" x 18"
60° angle
subcut 4½" parallelograms

4 D: 60 p. 20
1 strip 2½" x 18"
60° angle
subcut 2½" diamonds

4 E: 30 p. 19
2 strips 6⅞+"* (*halfway between 6⅞" and 7")
subcut 6⅞+"* squares
60° angle from corner
trim off 2nd corner to match 1st

red print for border
border: (abutted)
2 strips 3½" x 61" (sides)
2 strips 3½" x 53⅛" (top/bottom)

folded binding
16 strips 2" x 18"

lining fabric
2 panels 28⅝" x 70½"

Construction

Make 36 W units as shown, attaching the center triangle of each block using a partial seam (page 93).

Make 4 rows of 9 units as shown in the quilt diagram. Add a C to one end of each row and a Cr to the other end. Join rows.

Attach gold border strips to sides then top and bottom. Make 34 X, 34 Y, and 4 Z units. Join 7 X, 1 Z, and 7 Y; add an E patch to each end for top border. Repeat for bottom. Join 10 X, 1 Z, and 10 Y for each side border. Attach pieced borders, setting in corners (page 145).

Mark the fern motifs in B, C, and Cr patches in quilt center. Mark the motif from page 92 in the outer border. Quilt as marked. Quilt in the ditch around outside of pinwheels and around border B and Br parallelograms, extending lines through the inner borders. Quilt in the ditch between quilt center and inner border and between pieced border and outer border. Bind to finish.

Quilt Diagram

36 W

W piecing

See p. 93, partial seams

4 Z

Z piecing

34 X

X piecing

34 Y

Y piecing

Quilting

97

Horn of Plenty

What Was I Thinking?

Horn of Plenty is my own variation of the traditional 1000 Pyramids design. I was contemplating simple patterns that might look good embelllished with a Smattering of Stars. 1000 Pyramids was the perfect candidate. I simply substituted 60° diamonds for some of the triangles in order to make stars.

When I sent the pattern off to Candace Carmichael, I told her what I had done and suggested that she do something different. She certainly did! She found another pattern altogether lurking beneath the surface of the one I sent. By placing the strongest colors in the triangles around each star, she really brought out the stars.

Quiltmakers' Style & Color Choices

This is a simple design, even with the addition of stars. In order to add another layer of interest, I employed fluid colors. The values flow from light tones at the top to dark shades at the bottom of the quilt. This shift of value extends into the pieced and plain borders, as well.

In my version, the stars are subtle because they are made from the same colors as the background triangles. They are also regularly spaced.

The stars are more pronounced in Candace's version because of their contrasting colors. They are sprinkled randomly in that version and in diagonal rows in mine. Candace used cooler colors and added more stars.

Ideas for Taking Horn of Plenty Further

Both versions were made in twin size. For a queen-sized quilt, make 14 rows of 23 units each, plus borders. For a baby quilt or wall quilt, make 8 rows of 11 units each, plus borders.

Color Country Chords in straightforward darks and lights instead of using fluid colors. This simplifies the thinking. Use the blue and cream scrap color scheme from Shakespeare in the Park (page 80). If you prefer, use the color scheme from the smaller Shakespeare in the Park quilt. Make the stars from black and gold diamonds to stand out against background triangles of red and cream.

Use the color scheme from Wilderness Log Cabin on page 114. Color the background with scrappy darks and lights; color the stars in purple and rust.

Try using a single background fabric and scrappy darks to contrast as in the Acrobatik quilt on page 95.

The quilts on pages 38 and 65 also have colors and fabrics suitable for this pattern.

Quilt concentric quarter circles in a Fan pattern all over the quilt, as in the 9-Patch variation on page 119. Or quilt in the ditch around the stars and borders, and quilt the spiral motif from page 126 over the background triangles.

Piece 'n' Play with the units to decide where to place the Smattering of Stars. Try placing them around the edges of the quilt center or in a medallion-like ring to see what you like best.

Ideas to Be Gleaned From Horn of Plenty

Add a Smattering of Stars to any simple quilt. Simple patterns provide wonderful backdrops for stars to shine.

Highlight a star with a halo of color around it as on page 104. Or make stars subtle by changing only the shapes, not the colors, of the patches, as seen on page 100.

Use a design wall to plan fluid colors that gradually change across the surface of the quilt center and even into the borders.

Cutting and Sewing Considerations

You'll need a ruler with a 60° angle for this quilt. (Most decent rulers have them.) The shapes may be new to you, but they're easy to cut and sew.

The color shifts at the edge of the lightest and darkest star blocks. Make star units into half star blocks. Each row is the width of a half star, so don't join halves until you stitch rows to one another. Press seam allowances to oppose those of neighboring units. Read the tips on trimming points of 60° patches on page 36.

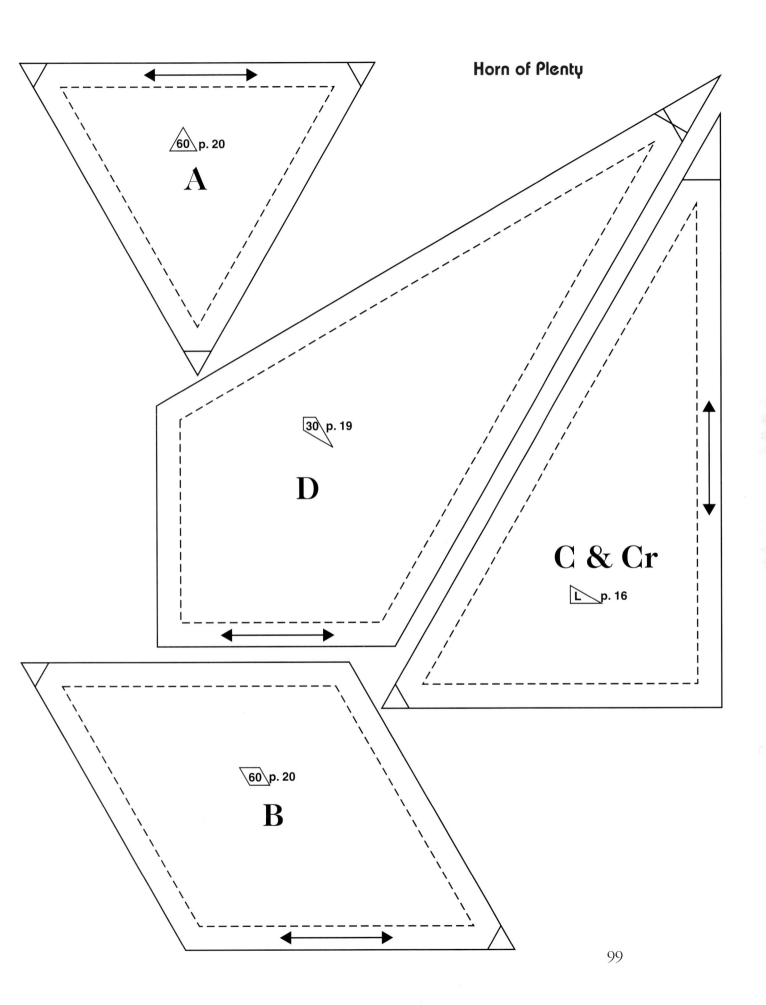

60 p. 20

A

30 p. 19

D

C & Cr

L p. 16

60 p. 20

B

Horn of Plenty
Country Chords

 Designed and pieced by Judy Martin; quilted by Jean Nolte, 1999. Scraps are sorted into five shades. At the top of the quilt, shades #1 and #3 (the lightest and the middle shades) are paired. In the middle of the quilt, shades #2 and #4 are used. The bottom of the quilt features shades #3 and #5. Shading extends into the borders, as well. A design wall is needed to execute this plan. For an easier version, sort scraps simply into lights and darks, ignoring the flow of color here. Batting is 100% cotton with scrim from Hobbs.

Quilt Size: 73¾" x 91"
Fits: twin bed
Set: 17 x 14 units
Requires:
14 L units
18 M units
20 N units
18 O units
36 P units
36 Q units
15 R units
15 S units
18 T units
14 U units

20 V units
18 W units
36 X border units
20 Y border units
36 Z border units
Cross References:
60° triangles (p. 20)
long triangles (p. 16)
60° diamonds (p. 20)
30° kites (p. 19)
design wall (p. 6)
sixteenths (p. 23)
reversals (p. 22)
4 set-in seams (p. 145)

Yardage		
yds.	**or**	**fat qtrs.**
1¾	light prints	7
1¾	med. lt. prints	7
3¼	med. prints	13
1¾	med. dk. prints	7
1¾	dark prints	7
¾	binding	3
5¾	lining	25
78" x 95" batting		

Cutting

light prints, value #1
border: (abutted)
4 strips 3" x 18" (inner top)
3 strips 3⅜" x 18" (inner sides)

172 A: /60\ p. 20
22 strips 3¼" x 18"
60° angle
subcut 3¼" diamonds
cut in half

18 B: \60\ p. 20
5 strips 3" x 18"
subcut 3" diamonds

4 C: L\ p. 16
1 strip 3½+"* x 18"
subcut rectangles 6⅛+"*
cut in half

1 Cr (fabric face down): L\ p. 16
1 strip 3½+"* x 18"
subcut rectangle 6⅛+"*
cut in half

2D: /30\ p. 19
1 strip 5⅞+"*
subcut 5⅞+"* squares
60° angle from corner
trim off 2nd corner to match 1st

medium light prints, value #2
border: (abutted)
4 strips 3⅜" x 18" (inner sides)

214 A: /60\ p. 20
27 strips 3¼" x 18"
60° angle
subcut 3¼" diamonds
cut in half

15 B: \60\ p. 20
4 strips 3" x 18"
subcut 3" diamonds

3 C: L\ p. 16
1 strip 3½+"* x 18"
subcut rectangles 6⅛+"*
cut in half

3 Cr (fabric face down): L\ p. 16
1 strip 3½+"* x 18"
subcut rectangle 6⅛+"*
cut in half

medium prints, value #3
border: (abutted)
4 strips 3" x 18" (inner bottom)
3 strips 3⅜" x 18" (inner sides)
9 strips 3½" x 18" (outer top, sides)

*halfway between listed number and next higher ⅛"

284 A: △60 p. 20
36 strips 3¼" x 18"
60° angle
subcut 3¼" diamonds
cut in half

74 B: ⟍60⟍ p. 20
19 strips 3" x 18"
subcut 3" diamonds

6 Cr (fabric face down): ◣ p. 16
2 strips 3½+"* x 18"
subcut rectangle 6⅛+"*
cut in half

2 D: ◺30 p. 19
1 strip 5⅞+"*
subcut 5⅞+"* squares
60° angle from corner
trim off 2nd corner to match 1st

medium dark prints, value #4
border: (abutted)
4 strips 3½" x 18" (outer sides)

174 A: △60 p. 20
22 strips 3¼" x 18"
60° angle
subcut 3¼" diamonds
cut in half

35 B: ⟍60⟍ p. 20
9 strips 3" x 18"
subcut 3" diamonds

3 C: ◣ p. 16
1 strip 3½+"* x 18"

subcut rectangles 6⅛+"*
cut in half

3 Cr (fabric face down): ◣ p. 16
1 strip 3½+"* x 18"
subcut rectangles 6⅛+"*
cut in half

dark prints, value #5
border: (abutted)
9 strips 3½" x 18" (outer sides/bot.)

96 A: △60 p. 20
12 strips 3¼" x 18"
60° angle
subcut 3¼" diamonds
cut in half

56 B: ⟍60⟍ p. 20
14 strips 3" x 18"
subcut 3" diamonds

4 C: ◣ p. 16
1 strip 3½+"* x 18"
subcut rectangles 6⅛+"*
cut in half

1 Cr (fabric face down): ◣ p. 16
1 strip 3½+"* x 18"
subcut rectangle 6⅛+"*
cut in half

folded binding
21 strips 2" x 18"

lining fabric
2 panels 39¼" x 95"

*halfway between listed number and next higher ⅛"

Construction

See the unit and quilt diagrams on the facing page. Make units in the quantities listed. Arrange as shown. Join 17 units to make a row. Add a C to one end and a Cr to the opposite end. Make 14 rows. Join rows to finish the quilt center.

Join strips to make plain borders, changing shades to correspond with the quilt center. Inner and outer border strips are identified in the cutting directions. Add inner borders to sides, then top and bottom. Make left pieced border from 1 N, 2 X, 10 Y, and 14 Z

units. Make right pieced border from 14 X, 10 Y, 2 Z, and 1 V. Attach both side borders. Make top border from 20 X, 1 N and a D patch at each end. Make bottom border from 20 Z, 1 V and a D at each end. Attach both. Add outer side, then top/bottom borders.

I quilted large, improvised feathers. If you prefer a pattern, quilt the Daisy (page 174) in the stars. Quilt in the ditch between patches. Stipple quilt C and Cr patches and inner border. Extend lines from the diamonds into the outer border. Bind to finish.

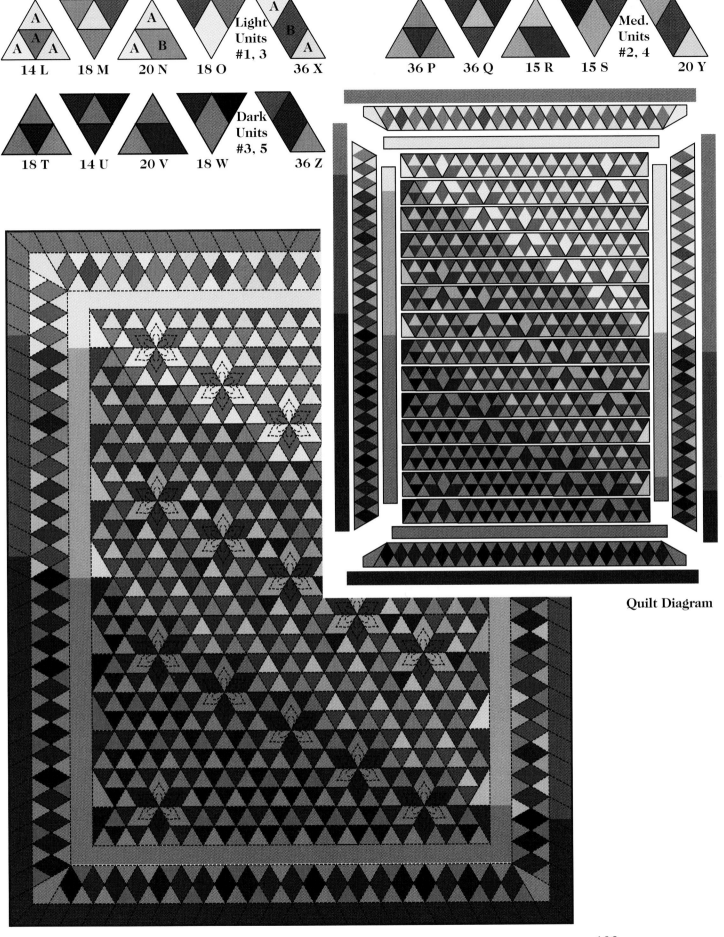

14 L 18 M 20 N 18 O Light Units #1, 3 36 X

Med. Units #2, 4
36 P 36 Q 15 R 15 S 20 Y

Dark Units #3, 5
18 T 14 U 20 V 18 W 36 Z

A A A
A B
A B A

Quilt Diagram

Quilting

103

Horn of Plenty
Cool Jewel

 Designed by Judy Martin; pieced by Candace Carmichael, 1999. Candace placed stars randomly here, whereas I placed stars in a regular arrangement in my version. Candace framed each yellow star with a darker star, which makes the yellow stars stand out. My stars were barely perceptible. Go strong, subtle, or anywhere in between in your own Horn of Plenty quilt. Design wall planning is imperative for this coloring.

Quilt Size: 73¾" x 91"
Fits: twin bed
Set: 17 x 14 units
Requires:
50 N units
50 O units
12 P units
12 Q units
21 R units
12 S units
12 T units
22 U units
12 V units

12 W units
23 X units
4 Y border end units,
92 Z border units
Cross References:
60° triangles (p. 20)
long triangles (p. 16)
60° diamonds (p. 20)
30° kites (p. 19)
design wall (p. 6)
4 set-in seams (p. 145)
reversals (p. 22)
sixteenths (p. 23)

yds.	Yardage or	fat qtrs.
2	light blues	8
1	medium blues	4
½	med. dk. blues	2
¾	dark blues	3
1	medium pinks	4
½	med. dk. pinks	2
1¾	dark pinks	7
1	med. purples	4
½	med. dk. purple	2
1	dark purples	4
½	med. yellows	2
½	dark yellows	2
¾	binding	3
5¾	lining	25
	78" x 95" batting	

Cutting

light blue and purple prints
300 A: ⟨60⟩ p. 20
38 strips 3¼" x 18"
60° angle
subcut 3¼" diamonds
cut in half

7 C: ⟨L⟩ p. 16
2 strips 3½+"* x 18"
subcut rectangles 6⅛+"*
cut in half

7 Cr (fabric face down): ⟨L⟩ p. 16
2 strips 3½+"* x 18"
subcut rectangle 6⅛+"*
cut in half

medium blue prints
124 A: ⟨60⟩ p. 20
16 strips 3¼" x 18"
60° angle
subcut 3¼" diamonds
cut in half

4 C: ⟨L⟩ p. 16
1 strip 3½+"* x 18"
subcut rectangles 6⅛+"*
cut in half

4 Cr (fabric face down): ⟨L⟩ p. 16
1 strip 3½+"* x 18"
subcut rectangle 6⅛+"*
cut in half

folded binding
21 strips 2" x 18"

medium dark blue prints
77 A: ⟨60⟩ p. 20
10 strips 3¼" x 18"
60° angle
subcut 3¼" diamonds
cut in half

dark blue prints
69 A: ⟨60⟩ p. 20
9 strips 3¼" x 18"
60° angle
subcut 3¼" diamonds
cut in half

31 B: ⟨60⟩ p. 20
8 strips 3" x 18"
60° angle
subcut 3" diamonds

medium pink prints
border: (abutted)
9 strips 3⅜" x 18" (sides)
8 strips 3" x 18" (top/bottom)

24 A: ⟨60⟩ p. 20
3 strips 3¼" x 18"
60° angle
subcut 3¼" diamonds
cut in half

lining fabric
2 panels 39¼" x 95"

*halfway between listed number and next higher ⅛"

105

medium dark pink prints

76 A: ⟋60⟍ p. 20
10 strips 3¼" x 18"
60° angle
subcut 3¼" diamonds
cut in half

dark pink prints

border: (abutted)
20 strips 3½" x 18"

63 A: ⟋60⟍ p. 20
8 strips 3¼" x 18"
60° angle
subcut 3¼" diamonds
cut in half

31 B: ⟍60⟍ p. 20
8 strips 3" x 18"
60° angle
subcut 3" diamonds

medium purple prints

124 A: ⟋60⟍ p. 20
16 strips 3¼" x 18"
60° angle
subcut 3¼" diamonds
cut in half

3 C: ⌊L⟍ p. 16
1 strip 3½+"* x 18"
subcut rectangles 6⅛+"*
cut in half

3 Cr (fabric face down): ⌊L⟍ p. 16
1 strip 3½+"* x 18"
subcut rectangle 6⅛+"*
cut in half

medium dark purple prints

77 A: ⟋60⟍ p. 20
10 strips 3¼" x 18"
60° angle
subcut 3¼" diamonds
cut in half

dark purple prints

66 A: ⟋60⟍ p. 20
9 strips 3¼" x 18"
60° angle
subcut 3¼" diamonds
cut in half

4D: ▱30⟍ p. 19
2 strips 5⅞+"*
subcut 5⅞+"* squares
60° angle from corner
trim off 2nd corner to match 1st

34 B: ⟍60⟍ p. 20
9 strips 3" x 18"
60° angle
subcut 3" diamonds

medium yellow prints

36 B: ⟍60⟍ p. 20
9 strips 3" x 18"
60° angle
subcut 3" diamonds

dark yellow prints

36 B: ⟍60⟍ p. 20
9 strips 3" x 18"
60° angle
subcut 3" diamonds

*halfway between listed number and next higher ⅛"

Construction

See the unit and quilt diagrams. Make units in the quantities listed. Arrange as shown. Join units 17 to a row. Add a C to one end and a Cr to the opposite end. Make 14 rows. Join rows to finish the quilt center.

Add light inner borders to sides, then top and bottom. Make a border from 26 Z units and 1 Y unit. Repeat. Sew to sides of quilt. Make top border from 20 Z and 1 Y. Add a kite-shaped D patch to each end. Attach. Repeat for bottom. Add plain dark borders.

Quilt the Daisy motif from page 174 in the yellow stars. Quilt the rest in the ditch between patches. Bind to finish.

50 N   50 O   12 P   12 Q   21 R   12 S   12 T   22 U   12 V   12 W   23 X   4 Y   92 Z

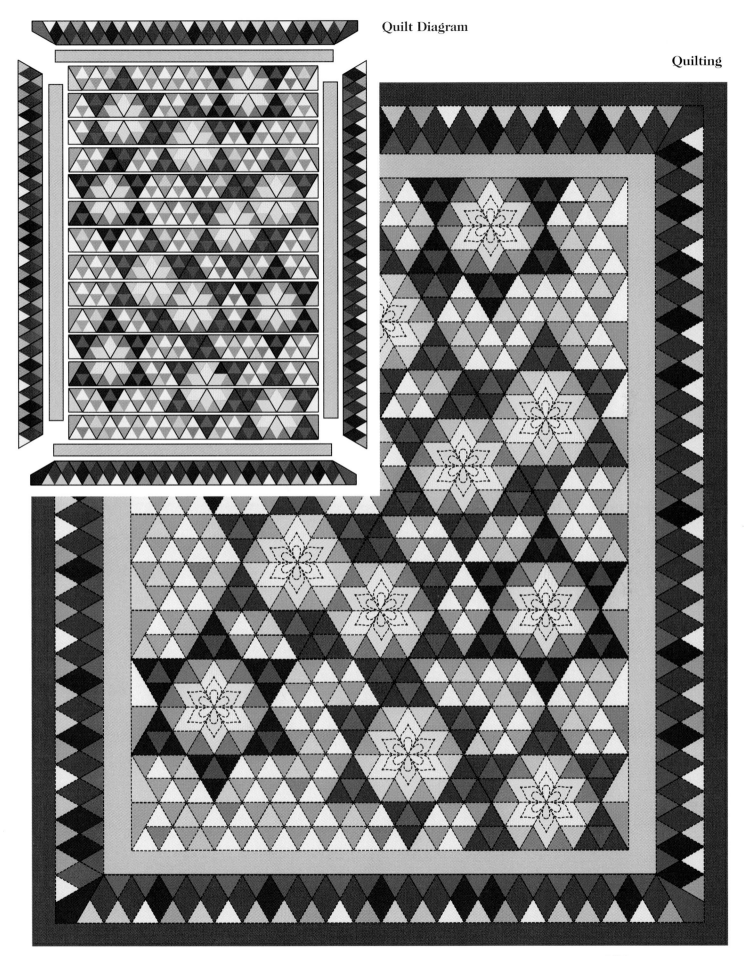

Quilt Diagram

Wilderness Log Cabin

What Was I Thinking?

I have been exploring the notion of incorporating a star in a Log Cabin since 1982. My most famous example is the Colorado Log Cabin first published in *Scrap Quilts*. That quilt has been very popular. However, I have always thought it was hard to make the star contrast with both light and dark logs as it must in that pattern. In this quilt, I wanted a dark star against the light half of the block for ease of contrast. This plan also adds a casual touch of asymmetry, which I like. The star in Wilderness Log Cabin is a simple variable star rather than a Le Moyne Star, so it requires no set-ins. Finally, only about a quarter of the blocks incorporate stars. The effect is one of a Smattering of Stars superimposed on a Log Cabin.

Quiltmakers' Style & Color Choices

I made my Wilderness Log Cabin in a vintage 1860s color scheme from current fabrics, including country prints and antique reproductions. Usually, I use solids for the small squares (called "cornerstones") dividing light and dark halves. However, here I used an assortment of barn red prints. For lights, I cut logs from butter yellow, tan, and pink; for darks, I cut logs from pumpkin, bubblegum pink, brown, and green. I cut star points and centers from bubblegum pink prints and pumpkin prints.

My quilt was quilted with straight lines, skewed in the quilt center.

Donna's version used scraps for logs, a single print for stars, and another print for cornerstone squares. Her light fabrics were similar to mine, but her darks were cooler, predominantly blue and green.

Donna stipple quilted the light areas and outline quilted the dark logs.

Ideas for Taking
Wilderness Log Cabin Further

For a twin-sized quilt, make 48 blocks set 6 x 8. Make pieced side borders as in the queen-sized quilt; for top and bottom borders, delete 4 stars from each. Adjust plain border widths to fit the border to the quilt. (Borders will need to be made in 2 widths.)

Consider making your Log Cabin in the colorwash style. Florals and whimsical prints can also be attractive. If you have a wide variety of scraps, it could be fun to make this log cabin with fluid color, as in the Horn of Plenty quilt on page 100.

The asymmetrical Log Cabin blocks, half light and half dark, can be turned myriad ways to make different patterns. Traditional arrangements include Barn Raising, Straight Furrows, Streak of Lightning, and Sunshine and Shadows, as illustrated in a few of my other Log Cabin quilt variations on pages 12–13. Almost 20 years ago I wrote an article for *Quilter's Newsletter Magazine* discussing the Log Cabin setting possibilities inherent in traditional quilt blocks. You can experiment on graph paper by representing a Log Cabin block as a single square divided diagonally into a light triangle and a dark triangle. When you do this, it is easy to see how you could derive arrangements from stars, pinwheels, and other motifs. The arrangement here incorporates a variable star in the center of a Barn Raising set.

You don't need to sketch on graph paper to come up with your own set. The Log Cabin block is perfect for what I call "Piece 'n' Play." Make the blocks. Then play with arranging and rearranging them before sewing the blocks into rows. This is an excellent way to arrange blocks with a Smattering of Stars.

You can place the star blocks in a formal, regular arrangement for a different look.

Ideas to be Gleaned
from Wilderness Log Cabin

Turn asymmetrical blocks to make different secondary patterns. Piece 'n' Play with the blocks before sewing them into rows.

Toss a few stars in for good measure. Be casual about their placement.

Cutting & Sewing Considerations

Cutting strips down to specified log lengths before sewing will help you sew accurately sized blocks. Note that the Log Cabin block having the star is pieced in a different sequence from the regular Log Cabin block.

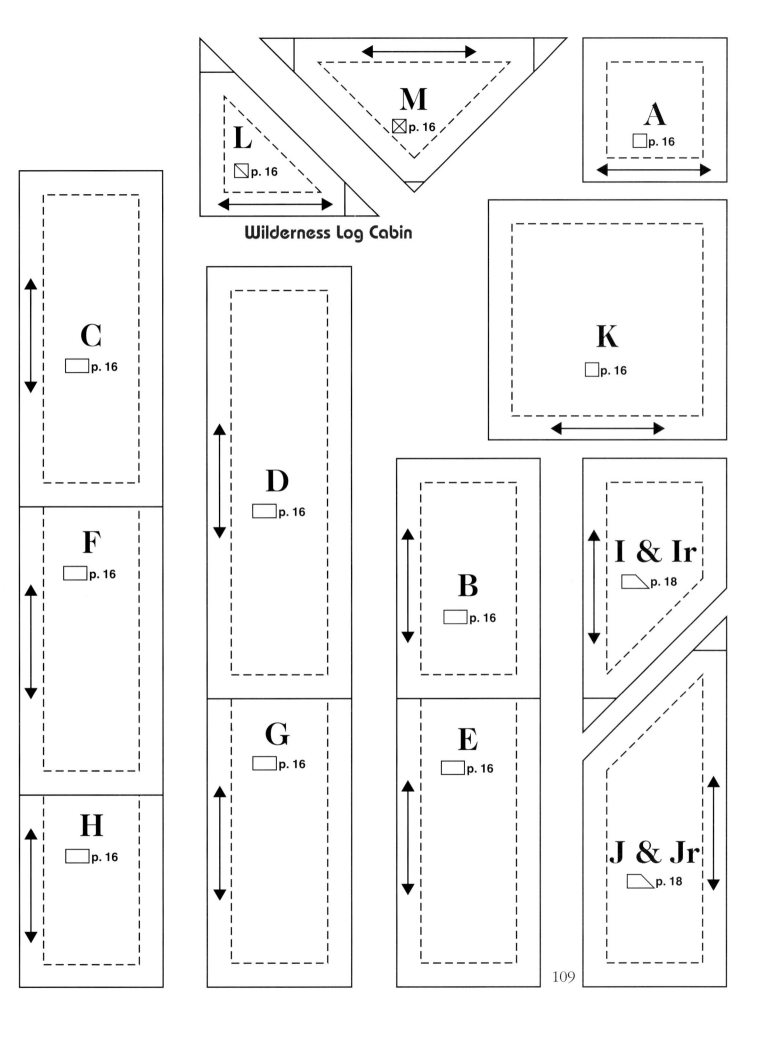

Wilderness Log Cabin

109

Wilderness Log Cabin
Thanksgiving

 Designed and pieced by Judy Martin; quilted by Jean Nolte, 1999. Fabrics include some Civil War prints by Judie Rothermel for Marcus Brothers and Everlastling Prints and Georgetown by Moda. A Smattering of Stars enhances some blocks and the borders. The stars are placed irregularly in the blocks and in a regular pattern in the border. The stars built into the Log Cabin blocks were inspired by my earlier Colorado Log Cabin design. However, here, the contrasts are easier to achieve, as the stars touch only the light logs. This is a fun Piece 'n' Play project. After making the blocks you can arrange and rearrange them to your heart's content. I used an arrangement consisting of a star center surrounded by a Barn Raising pattern. Quilting is in the ditch around stars, in parallel lines in the border background, and diagonally across the logs for a skewed effect. Batting is 100% cotton with scrim from Hobbs.

110

Quilt Size: 90" x 90"
Fits: double/queen bed
Block Sizes: 9" & 4" x 5"
Set: 8 x 8 blocks
Requires:
48 X blocks
16 Y blocks
80 Z blocks

Cross References:
Smattering of Stars (p. 13)
Piece 'n' Play (p. 12)
squares (p. 16)
rectangles (p. 16)
½ sq. triangles (p. 16)
¼ sq. triangles (p. 16)
½ trapezoids (p. 18)

Yardage		
yds.	or	fat qtrs.
6	light prints	24
4	dark prints	16
2	red prints	8
2	pink/pumpkin	8
¾	binding	3
8¼	lining	30
94" x 94" batting		

Cutting

light prints
You will need totals of 400 A, 48 B, 48 C, 160 D, 52 E, 48 F, 48 G, 64 H, 16 I, 16 Ir, 16 J, 16 Jr, & 352 M.

FROM EACH FAT QUARTER CUT

border: (abutted)
1 strip 2½" x 18" (x 19 fabrics)

11 A: ☐ **p. 16**
1 strip 1½" x 18" (x 24 fabrics)
subcut 1½" squares

4 D, 2 C, 2 B, 2 A: ☐ **p. 16** ☐ **p. 16**
2 strips 1½" x 18" (x 24 fabrics)
subcut rect. 4½", 4½", 3½", 2½", 1½"

2 E, 2 F, 4 A: ☐ **p. 16** ☐ **p. 16**
2 strips 1½" x 18" (x 24 fabrics)
subcut rectangles 5½", 6½", 1½", 1½"

2 G, 2 H: ☐ **p. 16**
2 strips 1½" x 18" (x 24 fabrics)
subcut rectangles 7½", 8½"

1 J, 1 Jr, 1 I, 1 Ir: ◹ **p. 18**
1 strip 1½" x 18" (x 16 fabrics)
subcut rectangles 3⅞", 3⅞", 2⅞", 2⅞"
cut off one end at 45° for half traps.

20 M: ⊠ **p. 16**
1 strip 3¼" x 18" (x 18 fabrics)
subcut 3¼" squares
cut in half along both diagonals

64 D: ☐ **p. 16**
1 strip 1½" x 18" (x 22 fabrics)
subcut 4½" rectangles

4 E: ☐ **p. 16**
1 strip 1½" x 18" (x 2 fabrics)
subcut 5½" rectangles

16 H: ☐ **p. 16**
1 strip 1½" x 18" (x 8 fabrics)
subcut 8½" rectangles

dark prints
You will need totals of
64 each of A through H.

FROM EACH FAT QUARTER CUT

4 C: ☐ **p. 16**
1 strip 1½" x 18" (x 16 fabrics)
subcut rectangles
3½", 3½", 3½", 3½"

4 B, 4 A: ☐ **p. 16** ☐ **p. 16**
1 strip 1½" x 18" (x 16 fabrics)
subcut rectangles and squares
2½", 2½", 2½", 2½",
1½", 1½", 1½", 1½"

4 F, 4 E, 4 D: ☐ **p. 16**
4 strips 1½" x 18" (x 16 fabrics)
subcut rectangles 6½", 5½", 4½"

4 G, 4 H: ☐ **p. 16**
4 strips 1½" x 18" (x 16 fabrics)
subcut rectangles 7½", 8½"

red prints
You will need a total of 576 A.

FROM EACH FAT QUARTER CUT

72 A: ☐ **p. 16**
7 strips 1½" x 18" (x 8 fabrics)
subcut 1½" squares

border: (abutted)
3 strips 2½" x 18" (x 8 fabrics)

pink or pumpkin prints

You will need totals of 96 K & 768 L.

FROM EACH FAT QUARTER CUT:

12 K: ☐ **p. 16**
2 strips 2½" x 18" (x 8 fabrics)
subcut 2½" squares

96 L: ◻ **p. 16**
6 strips 1⅞" x 18" (x 8 fabrics)

subcut 1⅞" squares
cut in half diagonally

folded binding
23 strips 2" x 18"

lining fabric
3 panels 32" x 94"

Construction

Make 48 X blocks, 16 Y blocks, and 80 Z blocks as shown. Place X and Y blocks in 8 rows of 8. Piece 'n' Play to find your favorite arrangement of blocks and stars. Join blocks to make rows. Join rows to complete the quilt center.

Join light border strips to make 2 borders 72½" long for sides and 2 borders 76½" long for top and bottom. Add light borders to sides, then top and bottom of quilt center.

Join 19 Z's to make a pieced border. Repeat to make 4 pieced borders. Sew 2 pieced borders to sides of quilt, with end stars away from the quilt center. Sew an E

to the side of each of the 4 remaining Z's. Sew one of these to each end of the top and bottom borders, as shown. Attach borders.

Join red border strips to make 2 borders 86½" long for sides and 2 borders 90½" long for top and bottom. Attach these borders to sides, then top and bottom.

Mark and quilt parallel lines 1" apart extending through the cream border, the background of the star border, and the red border. Quilt in the ditch around the quilt center and around star patches and red squares. Quilt straight lines from corner to corner of logs as shown. Bind to finish.

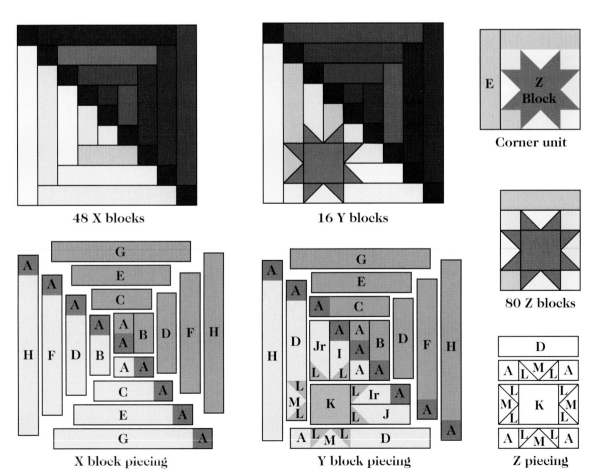

48 X blocks

16 Y blocks

E Z Block

Corner unit

80 Z blocks

X block piecing

Y block piecing

Z piecing

Quilt Diagram

Quilting

113

Wilderness Log Cabin
Indian Summer

 Designed by Judy Martin; made by Donna Davis, 1999. This is another example of a Piece 'n' Play quilt with a random Smattering of Stars. Donna came up with her own pleasing arrangement of Log Cabin blocks. Donna's stars are all one fabric, whereas mine were from scraps. She also used one fabric instead of scraps for the small accent squares. Donna outline quilted the dark logs and stipple quilted the light ones.

Wilderness Log Cabin: Indian Summer

Quilt Size: 50" x 50"
Fits: throw or wall quilt
Block Sizes: 9" & 4" x 5"
Set: 4 x 4 blocks
Requires:
12 X blocks
4 Y blocks
40 Z blocks

Cross References:
Smattering of Stars (p. 13)
Piece 'n' Play (p. 12)
squares (p. 16)
rectangles (p. 16)
½ sq. triangles (p. 16)
¼ sq. triangles (p. 16)
½ trapezoids (p. 18)

Yardage		
yds.	or	fat qtrs.
2¼	light prints	9
1	dark prints	4
1	purple print	4
1½	rust print	3
½	binding	2
3¼	lining	12
54" x 54" batting		

114

light prints

You will need totals of 180 A, 12 B, 12 C, 60 D, 16 E, 12 F, 12 G, 16 H, 4 I, 4 Ir, 4 J, 4 Jr, and 168 M. Some strips have mixed logs. Cut each strip into the lengths listed.

FROM EACH FAT QUARTER CUT

6–7* D, 20 A, 1–2* C: ▢ p. 16 ▢ p. 16
4 strips 1½" x 18" (x 9 fabrics)
subcut rectangles and squares
　4½", 4½", 1½", 1½", 1½", 1½", 1½"
　(*substitute 3½" rectangles for 12
　of the 4½" ones)

2 G, 2 F, 2 B: ▢ p. 16
2 strips 1½" x 18" (x 6 fabrics)
subcut rectangles 7½", 6½", 2½"

2 H, 2 E: ▢ p. 16
2 strips 1½" x 18" (x 8 fabrics)
subcut rectangles 8½", 5½"

1 J, 1 Jr, 1 I, 1 Ir: ◺ p. 18
1 strip 1½" x 18" (x 4 fabrics)
subcut rectangles 3⅞", 3⅞", 2⅞", 2⅞"
cut off end at 45° for half trapezoids
　and their reverses

20 M: ⊠ p. 16
1 strip 3¼" x 18" (x 9 fabrics)
subcut squares 3¼"
cut in half along both diagonals

dark prints

You will need totals of
16 each of A through H.
Strips have mixed logs.
Cut each strip into the
lengths listed.

FROM EACH FAT QUARTER CUT

4 C: ▢ p. 16
1 strip 1½" x 18" (x 4 fabrics)

subcut rectangles 3½", 3½",
　3½", 3½"

4 B, 4 A: ▢ p. 16 ▢ p. 16
1 strip 1½" x 18" (x 4 fabrics)
subcut rectangles 2½", 2½",
　2½", 2½", 1½", 1½", 1½", 1½"

4 F, 4 E, 4 D: ▢ p. 16
4 strips 1½" x 18" (x 4 fabrics)
subcut rectangles 6½",
　5½", 4½"

4 G, 4 H: ▢ p. 16
4 strips 1½" x 18" (x 4 fabrics)
subcut rectangles 7½", 8½"

purple print

44 K: ▢ p. 16
8 strips 2½" x 18"
　subcut 2½" squares

352 L: ◺ p. 16
20 strips 1⅞" x 18"
　subcut 1⅞" squares
cut in half diagonally

rust print

border: (abutted)
2 strips 2½" x 50½" (sides)
2 strips 2½" x 46½" (top/bottom)
　(or 12 strips 2½" x 18")

144 A: ▢ p. 16
4½ strips 1½" x 50"
　(or 14 strips 1½" x 18")
subcut 1½" squares

folded binding
14 strips 2" x 18"

lining fabric
2 panels 27¼" x 54"

Make 12 X blocks, 4 Y blocks, and 40 Z blocks as shown. Place X and Y blocks in 4 rows of 4. Piece 'n' Play to find your favorite arrangement of blocks and stars. Join blocks to make rows. Join rows to complete the quilt center.

Join 9 Z's to make a border. Repeat to make 4 such borders. Sew borders to top and bottom of quilt, with the end stars away from the quilt center. Sew an E rectangle to the side of each of the 4 remaining Z's. Sew one of these to each end of the side borders, as shown. Attach side borders. Finally add rust borders to top and bottom, then sides, to complete the quilt top.

Quilt in the ditch around purple star patches and rust squares. Outline quilt ¼" from one edge of dark logs as shown. Quilt light areas and borders with small meandering or stippling. Bind to finish. Sign, date, and enjoy!

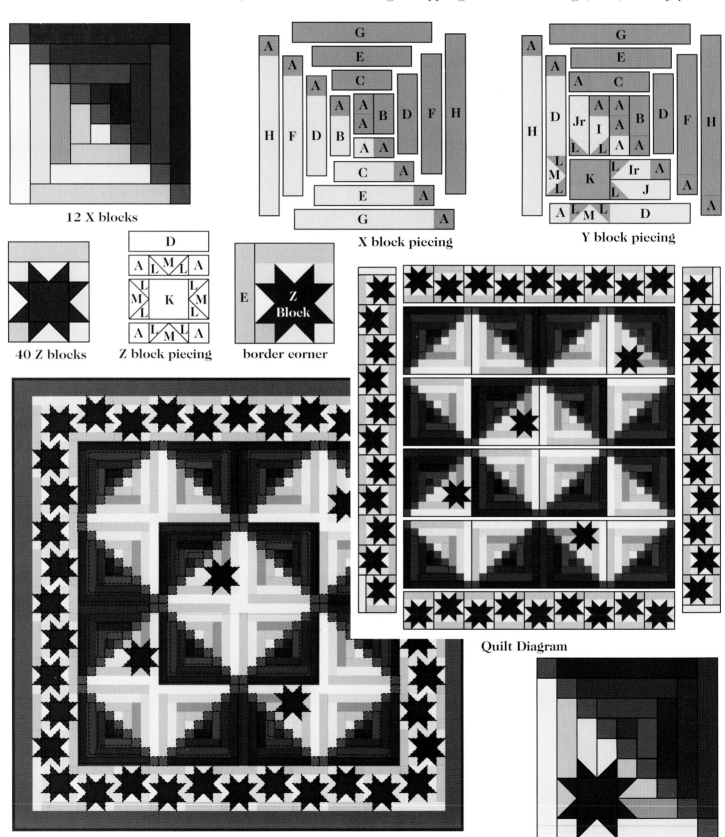

12 X blocks

X block piecing

Y block piecing

40 Z blocks

Z block piecing

border corner

Quilt Diagram

116

Quilting

4 Y blocks

9-Patch Variation

What Was I Thinking?

When I designed the Ontario Odyssey version of this quilt, my first thought was to combine zig-zag and barn raising arrangements for a Log Cabin block. (See Figs. 23–24 on page 12.) In order to get a suitable number of zigs and zags, I needed a small block. Rather than make tiny Log Cabins, I chose this simpler traditional block.

I wanted to keep the quilt interesting, so rather than making blocks uniformly half light and half dark, I made subtle changes to the colors in the lights and darks of each zig-zag band. I needed to map out my color sequence first, although you can simply follow my plan, if you like.

When I designed Countrytime with Lime, I was thinking about embellishing simple patterns with a Smattering of Stars. "Why not a Smattering of Leaves?" I thought.

Quiltmakers' Style Choices

In my low-contrast Ontario Odyssey quilt, the darks are lighter and the lights are darker than they are in Ardis Winters's Countrytime with Lime. Furthermore, my prints are busier. The effect in mine is somewhat impressionistic, whereas Ardis's is crisp like the autumn air. Ontario Odyssey was made in the mid '70s, and the colors and prints reflect that period. Countrytime with Lime is a new quilt with a fresh combination of vintage and country elements.

Countrytime with Lime is quilted with parallel diagonal lines in the dark areas and continuous-line spirals in the light areas. More spirals embellish the borders.

In contrast, Ontario Odyssey is quilted simply with Baptist Fans of concentric quarter circles.

Ideas for Taking
9-Patch Variation Further

For a twin-sized quilt measuring 72" x 96", make 192 blocks. Set them in 16 rows of 12 blocks each. The twin quilt will require about ¾ the yardage of the queen-sized quilt.

Try coloring leaves in bright fall colors and using light and medium light scraps for a subtly shaded 9-Patch background.

How about making this quilt a colorwash of busy light and dark patches?

For a warm colored quilt, follow the plan for Ontario Odyssey, but substitute the five values from the Horn of Plenty quilt on page 100, using shades #1 and 5 for Block V; #2 and 5 for W; #2 and 3 for X; #2 and 4 for Y; and #1 and 4 for Z.

If you prefer, use the design wall coloring plan from Horn of Plenty, with colors flowing from light through medium to dark as you go from the top to the bottom of the quilt. Pair #1 and 3 at the top; #2 and 4 in the middle; and #3 and 5 at the bottom.

Piece 'n' Play with blocks to find your favorite arrangement before stitching rows.

Ideas to be Gleaned from
9-Patch Variation

Not only Log Cabins, but any asymmetrical block can be a candidate for Piece 'n' Play. You can use the typical Log Cabin sets (pages 12–13) or devise your own.

Simple quilts become special when they are embellished with a Smattering of Stars. Other blocks, such as leaves, can also be used as accents. These blocks can be arranged in a regular pattern, as they are on page 123, or they can be placed randomly.

Any quilt can be quilted with the Baptist Fan quilting or Spirals quilting motifs presented with the two 9-Patch variation quilts.

Cutting & Sewing Considerations

This pattern is exceptionally easy to cut and sew. The Ontario Odyssey version has five different block colorings to keep track of, so it is something of a brain teaser.

For smooth lines between light and dark halves, join blocks as shown in the piecing diagram. If you can do it accurately enough for a smooth line, you may prefer to join light and dark triangles to form squares first, then join these units with squares to make three rows.

You can save time and yardage as you cut the trapezoids (C and Cr patches) for Countrytime with Lime if you have a Shapemaker 45 tool (S45). See page 18 for illustrated, step-by-step instructions.

117

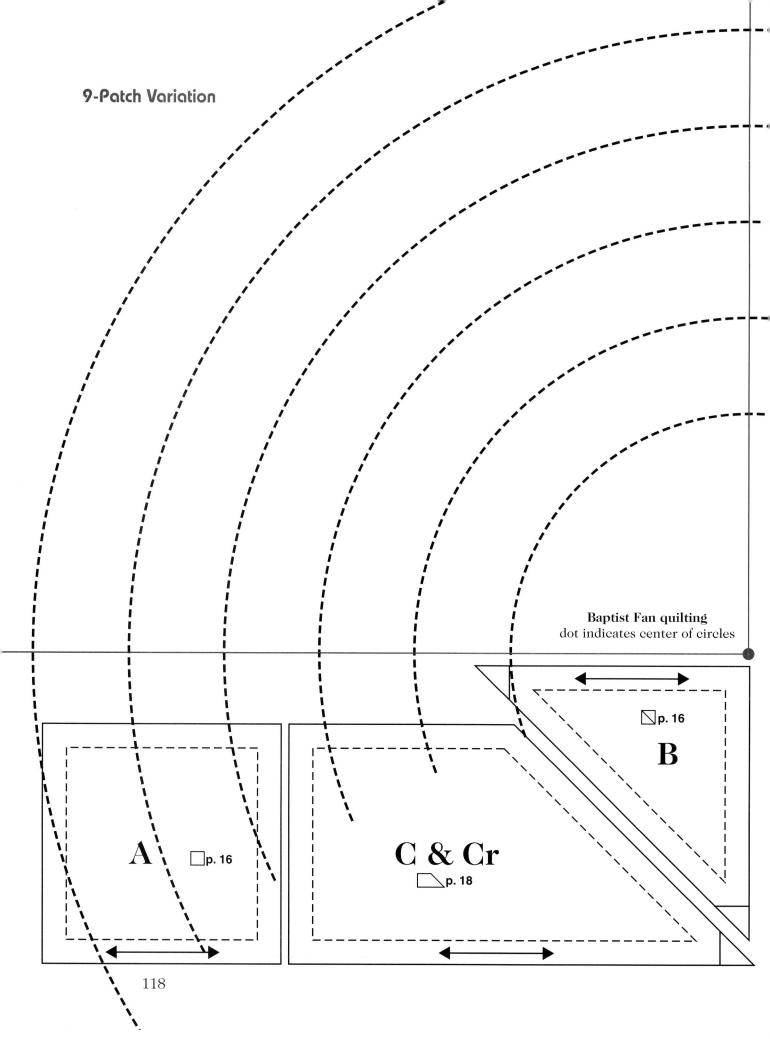

9-Patch Variation

Baptist Fan quilting
dot indicates center of circles

□ p. 16

B

A   □ p. 16

C & Cr
▱ p. 18

118

9-Patch Variation
Ontario Odyssey

Traditional design pieced by Judy Martin, 1977; quilted by Jean Nolte, 1999. (Note that it only took me 22 years to get this quilted!) I named the quilt to commemorate a canoe trip I made in 1972 from Lake Nipigon northeast toward James Bay. While this color scheme could be straight out of the 1930s, the fabrics are quintessentially '70s. Notice the way the busyness of the prints makes the quilt sparkle. The block is split diagonally into light and dark halves. This shading allows you to play with the block arrangement to create a variety of secondary patterns. This notion of making ordinary blocks and then messing around with their arrangement is loads of fun, and I call it Piece 'n' Play. The smaller block size of the 9-Patch Variation allows for more repetition, yielding some arrangements that would not be possible in a Log Cabin. Quilting in traditional Baptist Fan motifs completes the vintage look.

119

9-Patch Variation: Ontario Odyssey

Quilt Size: 96" x 96"
Fits: queen bed
Block Size: 6"
Set: 16 x 16 blocks
Requires:
76 V blocks
52 W blocks
84 X blocks
24 Y blocks
20 Z blocks

Cross References:
squares (p. 16)
½ sq. triangles (p. 16)
design wall plan (p. 6)
Piece 'n' Play (p. 12)

Yardage

yds.	or	fat qtrs.
1½	lt. blue prints	6
4	lt. green prints	16
2½	lt. pink prints	10
2½	blue prints	10
3¾	green prints	15
1¾	pink prints	7
¾	binding	3
8¾	lining	36
100" x 100" batting		

Cutting

light blue prints
144 A: ☐ p. 16
24 strips 2½" x 18"
subcut 2½" squares

144 B: ◺ p. 16
15 strips 2⅞" x 18"
subcut 2⅞" squares
cut in half

light green prints
384 A: ☐ p. 16
64 strips 2½" x 18"
subcut 2½" squares

384 B: ◺ p. 16
39 strips 2⅞" x 18"
subcut 2⅞" squares
cut in half

light pink prints
240 A: ☐ p. 16
40 strips 2½" x 18"
subcut 2½" squares

240 B: ◺ p. 16
24 strips 2⅞" x 18"
subcut 2⅞" squares
cut in half

folded binding
25 strips 2" x 18"

blue prints
236 A: ☐ p. 16
40 strips 2½" x 18"
subcut 2½" squares

236 B: ◺ p. 16
24 strips 2⅞" x 18"
subcut 2⅞" squares
cut in half

green prints
362 A: ☐ p. 16
61 strips 2½" x 18"
subcut 2½" squares

362 B: ◺ p. 16
37 strips 2⅞" x 18"
subcut 2⅞" squares
cut in half

pink prints
170 A: ☐ p. 16
29 strips 2½" x 18"
subcut 2½" squares

170 B: ◺ p. 16
17 strips 2⅞" x 18"
subcut 2⅞" squares
cut in half

lining fabric
3 panels 33¾" x 100"

Make blocks as shown below. Piece 'n' Play on a design wall or follow my plan. To recreate my quilt, see diagram on page 122. Start in the center with 4 V blocks. Around that place a ring of V blocks, followed by Z, Y, X, X, W, and V rings. (Note that the Y ring has X's in its corners.) Turn blocks as shown or as desired. Join 16 blocks per row. Join rows.

Mark fan motifs from page 118, placing the pink center dot over the lower left corner of the quilt for the first fan. Proceed to the right, placing center dots 8" apart at the edge of every fourth square. After the bottom row of fans is marked, mark a row of fans 8" above the first row. Rotate the pattern from the center dot if you need to extend the ends of the fan to touch the preceding fans. Quilt as marked. Bind to finish.

	light blues & greens
dark blues & greens	

76 Block V

	light pinks & greens
dark blues & greens	

52 Block W

	light pinks & greens
dark pinks & greens	

84 Block X

	light pinks & greens
dark pinks, blues & greens	

24 Block Y

	light blues & greens
dark pinks, blues & greens	

20 Block Z

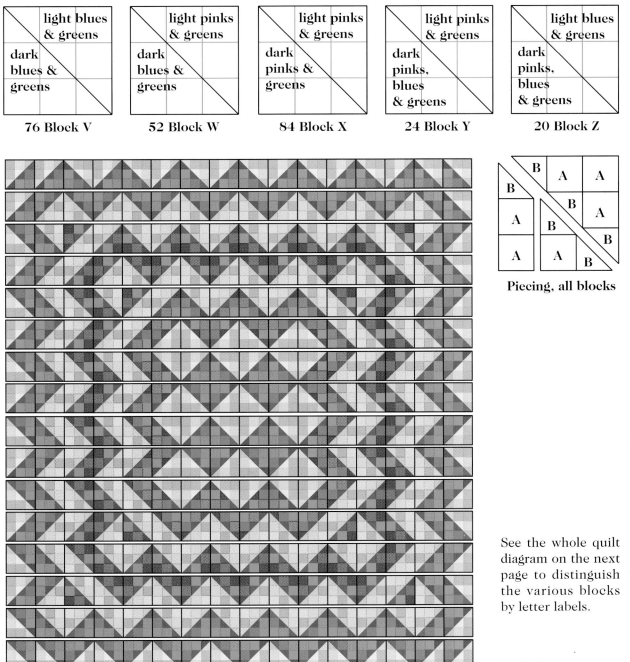

Piecing, all blocks

See the whole quilt diagram on the next page to distinguish the various blocks by letter labels.

Quilt Diagram

Lettered Quilt Diagram

V	V	V	V	V	V	V	V	V	V	V	V	V	V	V	V
V	W	W	W	W	W	W	W	W	W	W	W	W	W	W	V
V	W	X	X	X	X	X	X	X	X	X	X	X	X	W	V
V	W	X	X	X	X	X	X	X	X	X	X	X	X	W	V
V	W	X	X	X	Y	Y	Y	Y	Y	Y	X	X	X	W	V
V	W	X	X	Y	Z	Z	Z	Z	Z	Z	Y	X	X	W	V
V	W	X	X	Y	Z	V	V	V	V	Z	Y	X	X	W	V
V	W	X	X	Y	Z	V	V	V	V	Z	Y	X	X	W	V
V	W	X	X	Y	Z	V	V	V	V	Z	Y	X	X	W	V
V	W	X	X	Y	Z	V	V	V	V	Z	Y	X	X	W	V
V	W	X	X	Y	Z	Z	Z	Z	Z	Z	Y	X	X	W	V
V	W	X	X	X	Y	Y	Y	Y	Y	Y	X	X	X	W	V
V	W	X	X	X	X	X	X	X	X	X	X	X	X	W	V
V	W	X	X	X	X	X	X	X	X	X	X	X	X	W	V
V	W	W	W	W	W	W	W	W	W	W	W	W	W	W	V
V	V	V	V	V	V	V	V	V	V	V	V	V	V	V	V

Quilting

9-Patch Variation
Countrytime with Lime

Designed by Judy Martin; pieced by Ardis Winters; quilted by Jean Nolte, 1999. Judy combined elements of 9-Patch, Log Cabin, and Maple Leaf patterns to derive this new design. Ardis used her characteristic country flair when she chose scrappy prints in fall colors. The background and border quilting suggests swirling winds to go along with the falling leaves. The leaves are smattered here and there over the quilt in a regular pattern. Feel free to Piece 'n' Play with the blocks after you make them. Batting is a cotton blend by Hobbs.

9-Patch Variation: Countrytime with Lime

Quilt Size: 44" x 44"
Fits: crib or wall
Block Size: 6"
Set: 6 x 6 blocks
Requires:
27 Y blocks
9 Z blocks

Cross References:
squares (p. 16)
½ sq. triangles (p. 16)
½ trapezoids (p. 18)
Piece 'n' Play (p. 12)
Smattering of Leaves
 (p. 13)
reversals (p. 22)

Yardage		
yds.	or	fat qtrs.
1	cream prints	4
1¾	dark prints	7
½	green prints	2
½	binding	2
2⅞	lining	9
48" x 48" batting		

cream prints

81 A: □p. 16
14 strips 2½" x 18"
subcut 2½" squares

117 B: ◺p. 16
12 strips 2⅞" x 18"
subcut 2⅞" squares
cut in half

dark prints

borders: (abutted)
20 strips 2½" x 18"
cut into random lengths

81 A: □p. 16
14 strips 2½" x 18"
subcut 2½" squares

117 B: ◺p. 16
12 strips 2⅞" x 18"
subcut 2⅞" squares
cut in half

green prints

9 B: ◺p. 16
1 strip 2⅞" x 18"
subcut 2⅞" squares
cut in half

18 C: ◿p. 18
6 strips 2½" x 18"
subcut 4⅞" rectangles
cut off one end of each at 45° angle

9 Cr: (fabric face down) ◿p. 18
3 strips 2½" x 18"
subcut 4⅞" rectangles
cut off one end of each at 45° angle

folded binding

12 strips 2" x 18"

lining fabric

2 panels 24¼" x 48"

Construction

Make 27 Y blocks and 9 Z blocks. Piece 'n' Play to arrange them as desired in 6 rows of 6 blocks. Join blocks to make rows. Join rows to complete the quilt center.

Sew random 2½" strips together to make borders. Make 2 borders 36½" long, 4 borders 40½" long, and 2 borders 44½" long. Sew shortest borders to sides. Sew medium length borders to top and bottom. Sew remaining medium length borders to sides. Sew longest borders to top and bottom.

Mark and quilt the spiral motifs from page 126 in light block halves and borders. Quilt in the ditch around leaf patches and between light and dark halves. Quilt diagonal lines through dark squares. Bind to finish.

27 Block Y

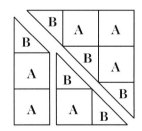

Block Y piecing

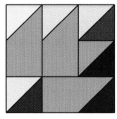

9 Block Z

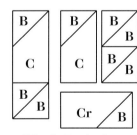

Block Z piecing

Border quilting, 2 repeats

124

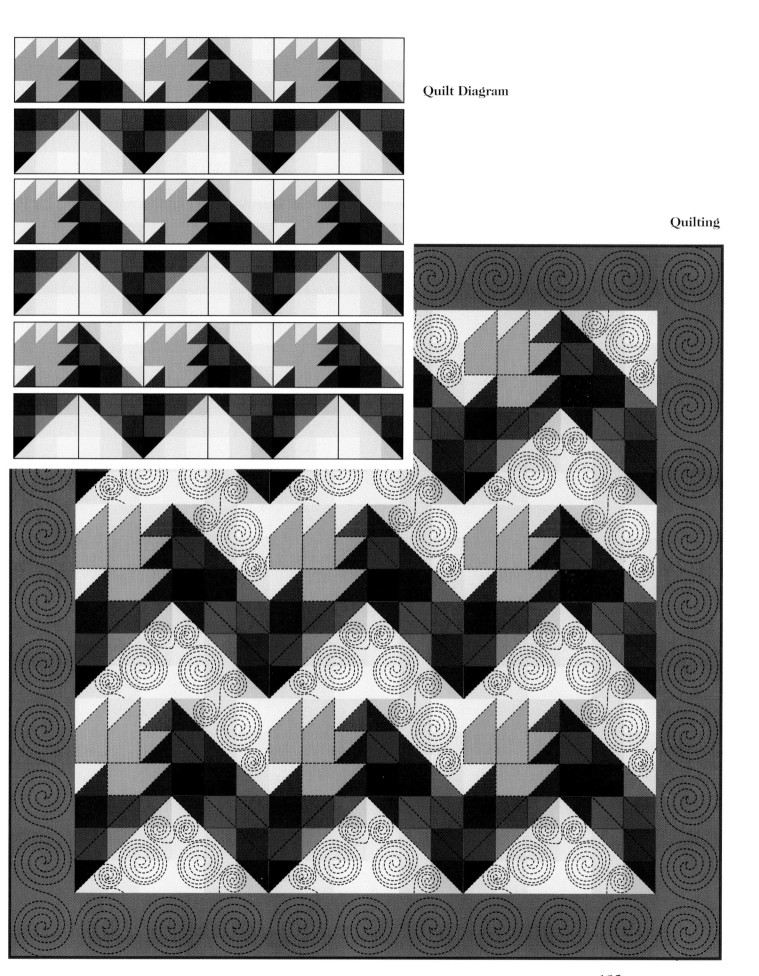

Quilt Diagram

Quilting

125

Prewash to Prevent Problems

My son has a new navy shirt that runs like a blue river every time it is washed. It doesn't get washed as often as he'd like, because I have better things to do with my time than wash a shirt separately. Imagine, though, the heartbreak if this fabric had been used in a quilt! After you have gone to all the trouble of cutting and sewing your quilt, there is no way to separate the light bits from the dark bits for laundering.

Prewashing is like quilt insurance, without all the premiums! It gives you peace of mind to know that your quilt will not shrink and its colors will not bleed. I test each fabric in the sink to see if it is colorfast. If the water stays clear, I then wash the fabric by machine with like colors and tumble dry to preshrink. I measure and trim ½" from the selvedge to eliminate markings and cupped edges. (Sometimes a little more than ½" is necessary.) After trimming off the selvedge, I go over each fabric thoroughly with a steam iron to smooth out wrinkles. (After cutting patches, I don't use steam.)

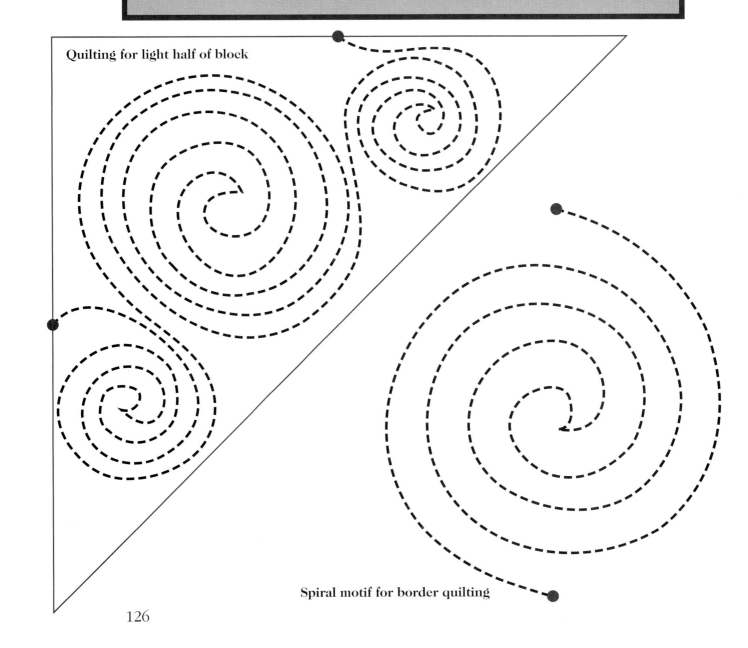

Quilting for light half of block

Spiral motif for border quilting

126

Judy's Maple Leaf

What Was I Thinking?

My friend, Chris, was having so much fun making a Maple Leaf quilt (Autumn Fantasy, page 136) that I couldn't help myself. I had to make one, too. I thought some of my readers might want an alternative to all those set-in joints, so I set out to make an easier block. (To be perfectly honest, I wanted to make the project easier on myself, too.) The standard Maple Leaf had that unnatural square in the middle that had always bothered me. I determined to eliminate the square as well as some other extraneous seams. My revised Maple Leaf has fewer patches, easier joints, and a more natural-looking asymmetry than the traditional Maple Leaf block.

Quiltmakers' Style & Color Choices

I knew I wanted the same kind of color shifting within the leaf that Chris was using so successfully in her quilt. Fall colors being what they are, I ended up with a palette similar to Chris's. Nevertheless, our personal taste in fabric overlaid our quilts with our own individual styles.

The biggest difference in colors between Chris's Autumn Fantasy and Judy's Maple Leaf is in the background. I chose a single fabric (Benartex Impressions by Patricia Campbell in her Fossil Fern motif) as opposed to Chris's scrap look in mixed values. This softens the bright color scheme. I made my Maple Leaf using batiks and contemporary fabrics. Leaf prints include many Bali Handpaints from Hoffman California Fabrics, as well as Red Sea from Kaufman.

Both quilts have staggered blocks for a more natural look. Autumn Fantasy has regular rows with a half block spacer at the left end of one row and the right end of the next. Judy's Maple leaf has four 6" leaves arranged with background rectangles to make a bigger, Grand Block. The big blocks were set side by side, turning one block thisaway, the next block thataway for a less rigid look.

Ideas for Taking
Judy's Maple Leaf Further

For a queen-sized quilt, make 25 blocks set 5 x 5. The quilt will measure 92" x 92".

Just 2–3 blocks make a handsome seasonal table runner or wall quilt. The narrow pieced border will make a striking frame.

Use the color idea from Autumn Fantasy, with mixed values in both the background and the foreground.

Delete the stems, as in Chris's quilt, for ease of sewing and a cleaner-lined look.

A gradated background fabric, such as that in the Grandmother's Wedding Ring quilt on page 38, would be perfect for Judy's Maple Leaf. I have seen the perfect print for this, a Nancy Crow print in gradated green or gold with leafy outlines.

Arrange leaves with darker ones at the bottom and lighter ones at the top, in the way colors flow in Horn of Plenty on page 100.

Colored differently, this block makes a dainty flower bud. Make the stem and two outside trapezoids green. Make the remaining trapezoid and triangle pink, yellow, or other flower color. This would be charming in '30s prints on muslin, such as the fabrics in the Texas Chain quilt on page 69.

Ideas to Be Gleaned From
Judy's Maple Leaf

Arranging small blocks into bigger blocks, as in Judy's Maple Leaf can result in complex looking arrangements that can be easily sewn. I call these units "Grand Blocks." They are a good way to get out of the rut of blocks lined up in rows.

Color schemes from the great outdoors always please. Autumn leaves or a garden in bloom can provide natural color inspiration.

A light background lightens the entire effect. To tone down brilliant colors, use a gentle background color.

Cutting & Sewing Considerations

I realize that some people avoid appliqué at all costs, so I offer your choice of pieced or appliquéd stems in Judy's Maple Leaf. These could also be eliminated altogether, as in Autumn Fantasy, page 136, if desired.

When cutting the half trapezoid shapes, you can save time and fabric by using the Shapemaker 45 tool. See instructions for half trapezoids on page 18.

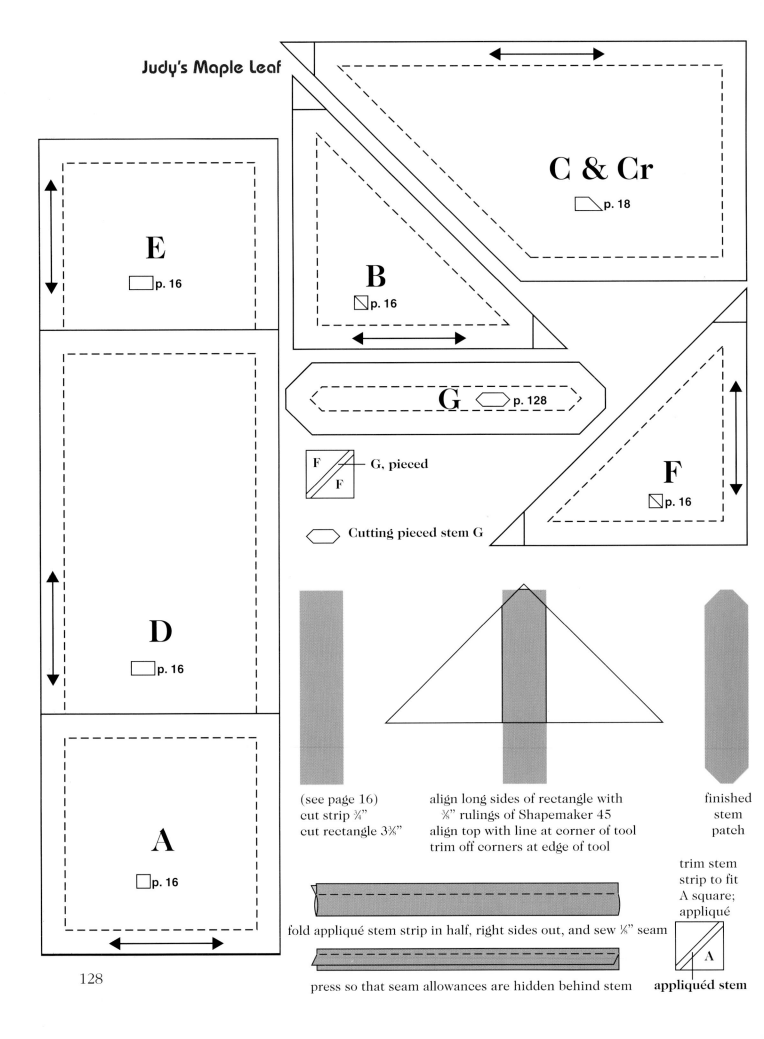

Judy's Maple Leaf

E   p. 16

C & Cr   p. 18

B   p. 16

G   p. 128

F   G, pieced

F   p. 16

Cutting pieced stem G

D   p. 16

A   p. 16

(see page 16)
cut strip ¾"
cut rectangle 3⅜"

align long sides of rectangle with
⅜" rulings of Shapemaker 45
align top with line at corner of tool
trim off corners at edge of tool

finished
stem
patch

trim stem
strip to fit
A square;
appliqué

fold appliqué stem strip in half, right sides out, and sew ⅛" seam

A

press so that seam allowances are hidden behind stem

appliquéd stem

Judy's Maple Leaf
Autumn Whisper

Designed and pieced by Judy Martin; quilted by Jean Nolte, 1999. This quilt features my own variation of a 6" Maple Leaf, joined four to an asymmetrical 14" block. My blocks are arranged in a regular pattern, but you may enjoy a Piece 'n' Play approach. A light background from Benartex keeps the quilt airy. Leaf fabrics include prints from Hoffman, Kaufmann, P & B, and Quilters Only. Batting is by Hobbs.

Quilt Size: 64" x 92"
Fits: twin bed
Block Size: 14"
Set: 3 x 5 blocks
Requires:
15 blocks
   made from 60 leaves

Cross References:
squares (p. 16)
rectangles (p. 16)
½ sq. triangles (p. 16)
½ trapezoids (p. 18)
reversals (p. 22)
Piece 'n' Play (p. 12)

Yardage

yds.		or	fat qtrs.
3*	dark prints		12*
*(or 2¾ yds./10 fat qtrs. using S45 tool)			
6	light print		23
¾	binding		3
5¾	lining		30
68" x 96" batting			

Cutting

dark prints for leaves

60 stems to piece or appliqué:

pieced stems:
60 G: ⬡ p. 128
12 strips ¾" x 18"
subcut 3⅜" rectangles
trim ends to make prism

   OR appliquéd stems:
   15 strips ¾" x 18"

184 B: ◺ p. 16
19 strips 2⅞" x 18"
subcut 2⅞" squares
cut in half

120 C: ◱ p. 18
40 strips 2½" x 18"
subcut 4⅞" rectangles
cut off one end of each at 45° angle
   (Important note: if you have an
   S45 tool, cut only 30 strips; cut
   half trapezoids at 4⅞".)

60 Cr: (fabric face down) ◹ p. 18
20 strips 2½" x 18"
subcut 4⅞" rectangles
cut off one end of each at 45° angle
   (Important note: if you have an
   S45 tool, cut only 15 strips; cut
   half trapezoids at 4⅞".)

light print for background

borders:
cut off piece 93¼" x 45" and cut into:
2 strips 7½" x 93¼" (mitered)
2 strips 7½" x 65¼" (mitered)
2 strips 2½" x 70½" (abutted)
2 strips 2½" x 46½" (abutted)

Cut leftover ends from 7½" border
   strips into 2½" strips. Use these
   and leftover 2½" border strip ends
   to cut the following:

30 D: ▭ p. 16
subcut rectangles 2½" x 6½"

Cut remaining yardage into 6 half-
   yard pieces from which to cut:

14 D (in addition to those above):
7 strips 2½" x 18"
subcut 6½" rectangle

120 F (if pieced stems): ◺ p. 16
10 strips 2⅝+"* x 18"
subcut 2⅝+"* squares
cut in half

60 A (if pieced stems): ▢ p. 16
10 strips 2½" x 18"
subcut 2½" squares

   OR 120 A (if appliquéd stems):
   20 strips 2½" x 18"   ▢ p. 16
   subcut 2½" squares

364 B: ◺ p. 16
37 strips 2⅞" x 18"
subcut 2⅞" squares
cut in half

15 E: ▭ p. 16
8 strips 2½" x 18"
subcut 8½" rectangles

folded binding

20 strips 2" x 18"

lining fabric

2 panels 34¼" x 96"

*halfway between listed number and next higher ⅛"

Piece or appliqué 60 stem/background units as shown on page 128. Make 60 leaves. Use these plus D and E patches to make 15 blocks. Arrange blocks in 5 rows of 3. Piece 'n' Play as you like. Join blocks and rows.

Add side, then top and bottom inner borders. Make 124 Z units. Join 37 Z's for each side border and 25 for top or bottom bor-

ders. Attach. Add wide borders, mitering each corner with a set-in seam (page 145).

Mark spirals from page 126 in large spaces between leaves. Mark and quilt leaves in wide borders. Quilt in the ditch around the dark patches and along edges of pieced borders. Quilt spirals, connecting them with small meandering stitching. Bind to finish.

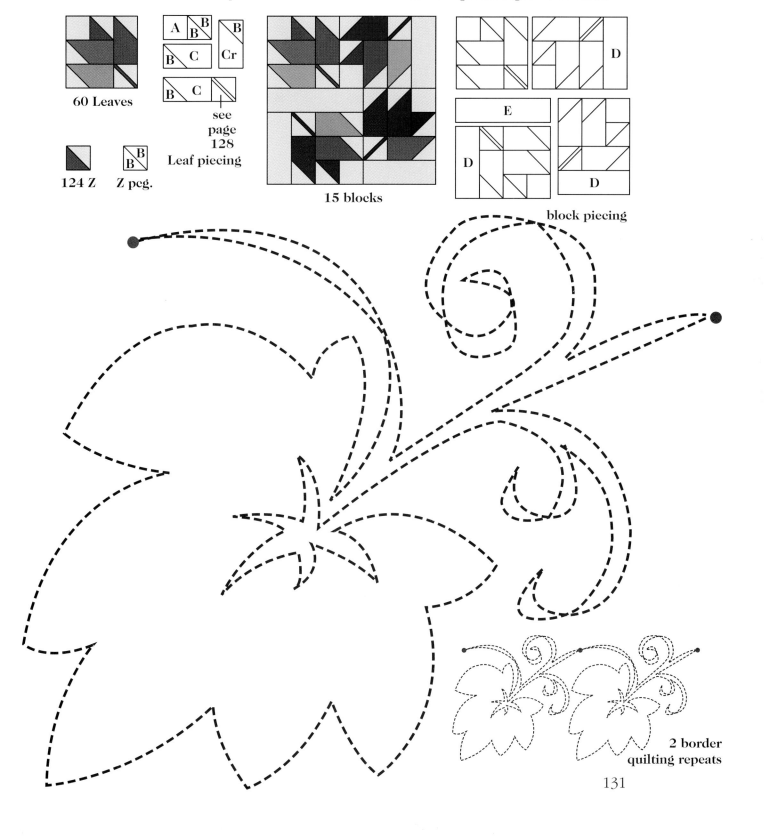

60 Leaves

A | B B

B C | B Cr

B C | see page 128

Leaf piecing

124 Z | **Z peg.**

15 blocks

D

E

D

D

block piecing

2 border quilting repeats

131

What Was She Thinking?

My friend, Chris Hulin, was excited about doing a fall quilt, but she wanted a more naturalistic shape than the standard Maple Leaf block. She combined elements of the standard block structure with her observations from actual leaves to come up with the basic block outline. Since then, we have seen other quilt blocks that were independently derived but used the same outline that Chris devised. Chris's block details take their cue from nature. The patch divisions suggest a vein extending upward from the stem and additional veins extending from the central vein toward the leaf tips. A square block center would have been easier to sew, but it would have looked less natural.

Chris decided on a staggered arrangement of blocks to avoid the unnatural regimentation of orderly rows. At first, Chris planned to use an arrangement of blocks and plain squares like that in Judy's Fancy (page 143). However, as Chris completed blocks and laid them out, it became apparent that there would be too much background in that arrangement. The leaves got lost. We played with the blocks, eventually arriving at the simple offsetting of the blocks from one row to the next. One row starts with a half-block space; the next row ends with the space.

Quiltmaker's Style Choices

Chris was planning her fall quilt as the leaves began to turn. The fall colors were glorious last year! Chris made a mental note of every color she saw; from flaming coral to lime green to deep plum. She clipped a photo from a magazine that had the color effect she sought. There were areas of brilliant color and deep shadow, and the leaves were indistinct, no more than an impression in places. Chris decided that a background of contrasting leaf colors best suited the quilt. Thus, some leaves would be dark against a light background and some would be light against a dark ground. Furthermore, Chris wanted to capture the moment of change by varying the color from one part of the leaf to another. So many of the actual leaves she studied were tinged with green, gold, or brown around the edges.

Chris gathered fabrics in the leaf colors she had observed and began cutting. After cutting a sufficient variety of patches, she began to lay out blocks. She quickly determined that fabrics with distinct, hard-edged prints were too abrupt. The best fabrics were batiks and marbles that had color gradations or subtle color shifts.

Some of the leaves were essentially monochromatic; others blended from one color into another. When all of the blocks were made and laid out in position, Chris cut the squares for the ends of the rows. These looked best in the more variegated prints.

The background/foreground ambiguity obscures the block outlines in places. The image seems to be a color impression rather than a picture per se. Then the leaf shape will assert itself in another area to reinforce the imagery of individual leaves.

Ideas for Taking
Autumn Fantasy Further

Autumn Fantasy can easily be converted to wall or queen size. For the wall quilt, simply make 4 rows of 4 blocks. The quilt will measure 37½" x 41¼", and you will need about ¼ the yardage of the twin size. For the queen quilt, make 11 rows of 11 blocks. You'll need more than 1½ times the yardage of the twin size.

Add appliquéd or pieced stems if desired. You can see how this was done in Judy's Maple Leaf on page 128. Note, however, that the background square is larger in the Autumn Fantasy quilt.

Piece 'n' Play. Have fun arranging blocks before you set them together.

Sun print fabric with actual leaves for a terrific background.

Use fluid color in the leaves, background, or both. Shifting the color from one area of the quilt to another is visually exciting and can simulate the play of light and shadow in nature. Chris found that she could make the colors flow best within a block by using batiks, hand-dyed fabric, and prints having areas of different colors blended together.

The Spiral quilting motif from page 126

could be used in the background and borders to heighten the windblown effect.

With the current rage for row quilts, you may like the idea of using one row of staggered Autumn Fantasy blocks as a part of a row quilt or strippie quilt. Do this in a Round Robin project or in a solo quilt.

Ideas to Be Gleaned From Autumn Fantasy

Several ideas from this quilt could be applied to other projects. The block coloring with its color shifts would be attractive in star patterns or pinwheels such as Grandmother's Flower Garden or Pinwheel.

The changing values of leaves and backgrounds from block to block could add excitement in other quilts as well.

The simple staggering of blocks seen in this pattern is an element that can work well in many other designs. Staggering blocks adds interest and naturalism here.

Simplifying a shape from nature or making a standard geometric pattern more natural are two other good ideas from this pattern that can be used in other quilts.

Cutting & Sewing Considerations

Note that each block has 3 set-in joints.

If you don't care to appliqué, you will be pleased to note that Chris has eliminated the stem in her pattern. If you're worried about such liberty-taking with nature, you can just say the stems decomposed!

For a fun, leisurely project, sew a block or two at a time after cutting plenty of patches.

Vein & stem quilting

134

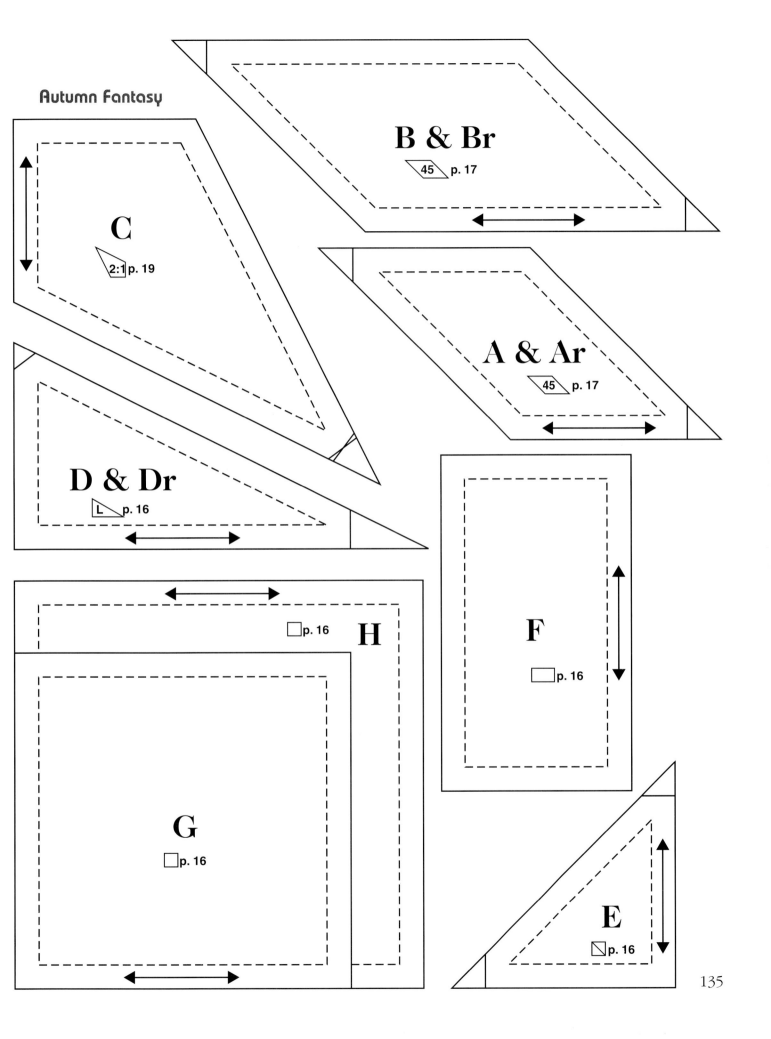

Autumn Fantasy

B & Br
45 p. 17

C
2:1 p. 19

A & Ar
45 p. 17

D & Dr
L p. 16

F
□ p. 16

H
□ p. 16

G
□ p. 16

E
◿ p. 16

Autumn Fantasy
Flagrantly Fall

 Designed and made by Chris Hulin, 1999. Chris's quilt won Best of Show at our local guild's show. Autumn Fantasy features the same fall colors and many of the same fabrics as Judy's Maple Leaf. However, Chris achieves an intensity of color by using the same fabric for background and leaves. Chris's block has set-in seams, but the more realistic effect is worth it. Blocks are turned randomly and staggered for a natural look.

Quilt Size: 63¾" x 90"
Fits: twin bed
Block Size: 7½"
Set: 7 x 11 blocks
Requires:
77 blocks
Cross References:
squares (p. 16)

rectangles (p. 16)
½ sq. triangles (p. 16)
parallelograms (p. 17)
long triangles (p. 16)
2:1 kites (p. 19)
231 set-in seams (p. 145)
Piece 'n' Play (p. 12)
sixteenths (p. 23)

yds.	Yardage or	fat qtrs.
5¾	leaves/borders	23
4	backgrounds	16
¾	binding	3
5½	lining	25
	68" x 94" batting	

Cutting

prints for leaves and borders

77 A: ⟍45⟍ p. 17
13 strips 2" x 18"
45° angle
subcut 1½+"* parallelograms
(*halfway between
1½" and 1⅝")

77 Ar: (fabric face down) ⟍45⟍ p. 17
13 strips 2" x 18"
45° angle
subcut 1½+"* parallelograms
(*halfway between
1½" and 1⅝")

154 B: ⟍45⟍ p. 17
39 strips 2" x 18"
45° angle
subcut 2⅝" parallelograms

154 Br: (fabric face down) ⟍45⟍ p. 17
39 strips 2" x 18"
45° angle
subcut 2⅝" parallelograms

77 C: ⟍2:1 p. 19
20 strips 3¾+"* x 18"
(*halfway between
3¾" and 3⅞")
subcut 3¾+"* squares
cut off corner at 2:1 angle
trim 2nd corner to match 1st

100 H: ☐ p. 16
25 strips 4¼" x 18"
subcut 4¼" squares

prints for backgrounds

77 D: ◣ p. 16
13 strips 2⁵⁄₃₂"* x 18"
(*2⁵⁄₃₂" is about 2 threads
bigger than 2⅛".)
subcut 4¼+"* rectangles
(*halfway between
4¼" and 4⅜")
cut in half diagonally

77 Dr: (fabric face down) ◢ p. 16
13 strips 2⁵⁄₃₂"* x 18"
(*2⁵⁄₃₂" is about 2 threads
bigger than 2⅛".)
subcut 4¼+"* rectangles
(*halfway between
4¼" and 4⅜")
cut in half diagonally

462 E: �₋ p. 16
33 strips 2⅜" x 18"
subcut 2⅜" squares
cut in half diagonally

154 F: ☐ p. 16
39 strips 2" x 18"
subcut 3½" rectangles

77 G: ☐ p. 16
20 strips 3½" x 18"
subcut 3½" squares

folded binding
20 strips 2" x 18"

lining fabric
2 panels 34¼" x 94"

Make 77 blocks, setting in patches at pink dots (see page 145). Arrange blocks in 11 rows of 7. Piece 'n' Play with the block orientations. Join blocks to make rows. Sew two H squares to each end of each row. Sew two more H squares to the right end of odd numbered rows and to the left end of even numbered rows. Join rows. Join 17 H squares in a row for the top border. Repeat for the bottom border. Attach borders. Mark veins and stems from page 134 in leaves. Quilt as marked. Outline quilt ¼" outside the leaves and ¼" inside the H squares. Bind to finish. Sign and date your masterpiece.

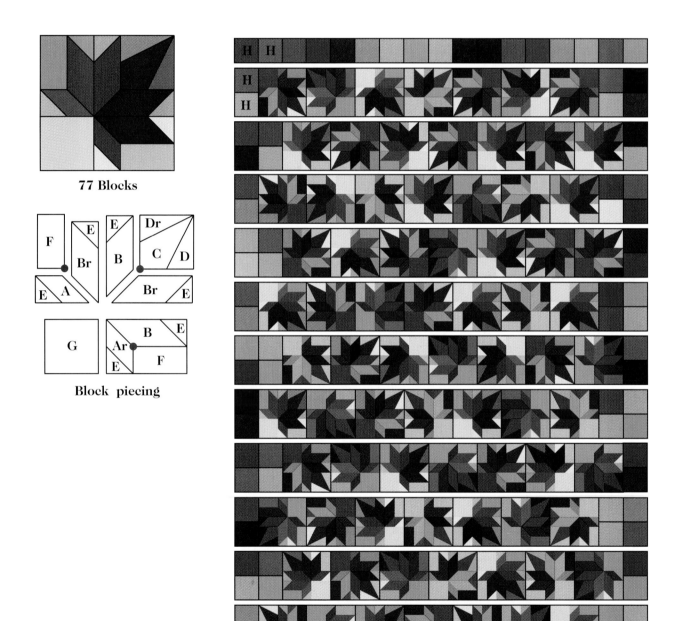

77 Blocks

Block piecing

Quilt Diagram

Quilting

Judy's Fancy

What Was I Thinking?

I came up with this design by starting with a small LeMoyne Star superimposed over the center of a larger LeMoyne Star. I split the background triangles in half with a seam in order to reduce the number of set-in joints. As long as I had a seam there, I figured I ought to mess with changing the color or fabric where those background patches meet. I saw the block divided into quarters, and it suggested a subtle checkerboard of scrap fabrics with the 3 background patches of a block quadrant matching.

The staggered block arrangement was a direct result of my laziness. I didn't want to join blocks point to point, so I offset them by half a block. What's the saying? Laziness is the mother of invention?!

I love the way these blocks go in unorthodox rows that do unexpected things around the edges. A built-in "border" of smaller LeMoyne Star blocks fills in and finishes the edges.

Quiltmakers' Style & Color Choices

I made Judy's Fancy in a vintage color scheme of black, red, bright yellow, blue, teal, bubblegum pink, brown, pine green, and cream. Each block was designed and made from its own set of fabrics. Background fabrics are mostly Marsha McCloskey's Staples from Fasco. Darker prints include antique reproductions and current fabrics. Old-Fashioned Ingenuity is bordered with a Smattering of LeMoyne Star blocks in an orderly arrangement.

Chris made her Sleek & Scrappy version in batiks and contemporary prints in a rainbow of vibrant colors. As with my version, each block was designed and made from its own set of fabrics. Chris substituted other fabrics liberally for the main fabrics in a block. This adds nuances of color. The background color is fluid, changing gradually from one corner to the opposite corner. The upper left corner is lighter and warmer; the lower right is darker and cooler.

This version has just a few LeMoyne star accent blocks sprinkled randomly over the quilt surface.

Ideas for Taking Judy's Fancy Further

Judy's Fancy patterns are presented in twin and queen sizes. For wall and double sizes, refer to the All Star patterns that start on page 151. The blocks for the two quilts are interchangeable, and the sets are the same pattern in different sizes.

The Smattering of Stars makes this quilt a great candidate for Piece 'n' Play. Before you stitch the rows, try different arrangements of big and small stars.

Consider making the large G squares from contrasting fabric rather than background prints. The All Star Savannah quilt on page 154 was done this way.

Alternative styles and color schemes that would make appealing Judy's Fancy quilts can be seen on pages 46, 65, 73, or 100. Amish, Lodge Look, Japanese, or Country styles would all work well in this quilt.

Ideas to Be Gleaned From Judy's Fancy

The smattering of smaller stars in a regular or irregular pattern over the quilt is an idea that can add excitement to many quilts.

The staggered arrangement will add freshness to other patterns. It may also get you thinking about other new ways to arrange blocks. Piecing from half-block rows makes staggered sets as easy to construct as ordinary sets.

The two Judy's Fancy quilts and the two All Star quilts are all made with a different set of fabrics for each block. This kind of scrap quilt is especially fun to make, and the idea could be used for any scrap quilt.

The Sleek & Scrappy quilt on page 147 was planned on a design wall with colors that change from one corner to the other. This kind of coloring can be used for any quilt. It adds a contemporary flair to a project.

Old-Fashioned Ingenuity has brillliant touches of color to perk up the quilt. Intense reds and yellows in small doses can be easily introduced in a scrap quilt without going overboard. Try this in your next scrap quilt for a lively spark.

Substitute slightly mismatched patches in a block for personality and the illusion of depth. You can do this in any quilt. Pretend you have run out of the main fabric and are making do. It is very freeing! Chris did this in her Judy's Fancy, and it adds a layer of complexity to the imagery.

Cutting & Sewing Considerations

This quilt pattern is not for everybody. It has many set-in joints and an arrangement that requires a design wall or a thinking cap. Nonetheless, half of the set-in seams in the bigger blocks are eliminated, so the quilt is easier than it might have been.

The 10¼" block size may sound odd, but it was chosen because the rotary-cut patches are 7 times more accurate in this size than they are in the customary 12" block size.

The All-Star quilt on page 154 utilizes the same set, and the same 10¼" block size, but the blocks have no set-ins. This would be a good alternative if set-ins intimidate you at this point in your learning curve.

Note that the block halves are not joined until the rows are joined. This makes piecing a breeze.

Judy's Fancy is a good quilt to make piece-meal. You can plan, cut, and sew 1–4 blocks at a time for a comfortably-paced project.

Judy's Fancy

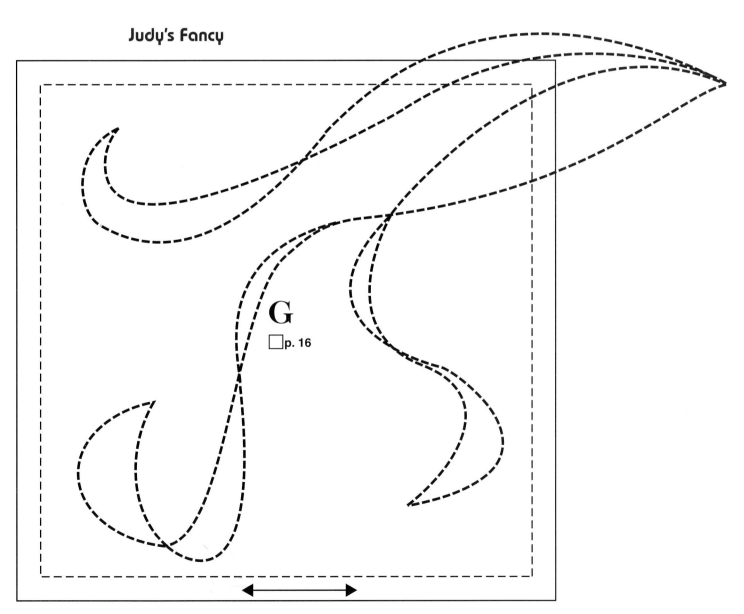

G
☐ p. 16

141

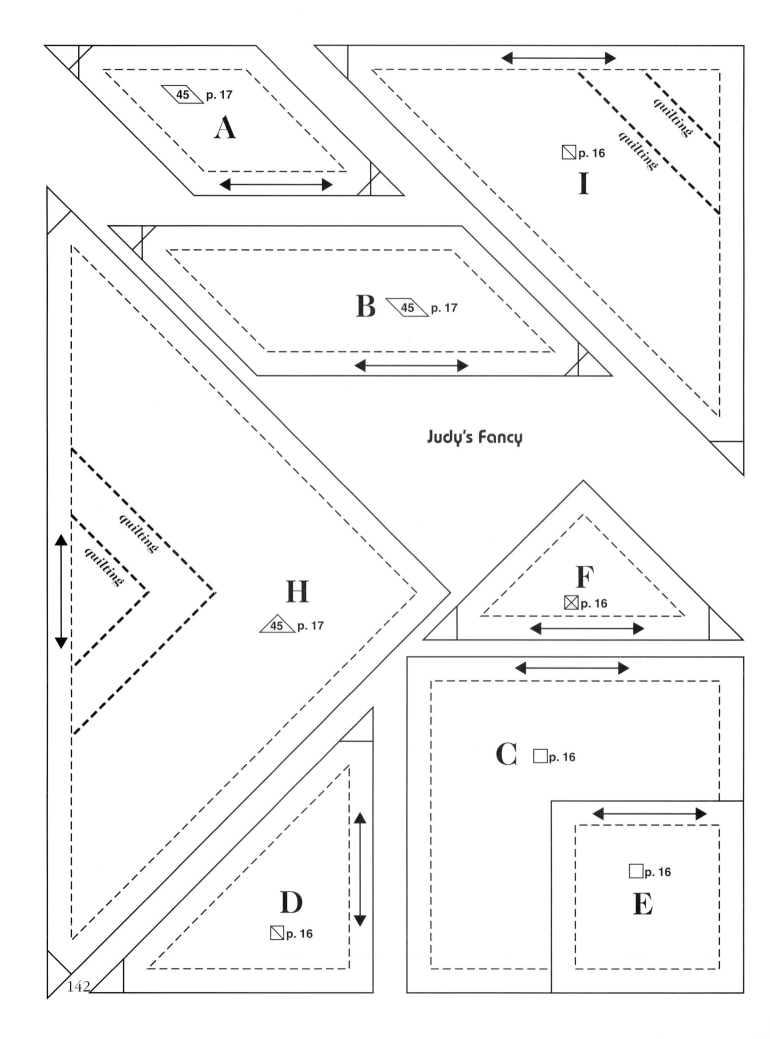

A
45 p. 17

I
p. 16
quilting
quilting

B
45 p. 17

Judy's Fancy

H
45 p. 17
quilting
quilting

F
p. 16

C
p. 16

D
p. 16

E
p. 16

142

Judy's Fancy
Old-Fashioned Ingenuity

Designed and pieced by Judy Martin; quilted by Barbara Ford, 1995. Judy chose a vintage 1860s color scheme and many reproduction fabrics for this quilt. The smaller stars are placed regularly around the quilt's edges. Half blocks are made and joined in diagonal rows to achieve the look of staggered blocks. A design wall is helpful here. Background fabrics are primarily Staples by Marsha McCloskey, courtesy of Fasco.

Quilt Size: 63⅛" x 84⅞"
Fits: twin bed
Block Size: 10¼" x 5⅛"
Border Block Size: 5⅛"
Requires:
50 Y units
28 Z units
Cross References:
45° parallelograms (p. 17)

45° diamonds (p. 17)
squares (p. 16)
¼ sq. triangles (p. 16)
½ sq. triangles (p. 16)
45° triangles (p. 17)
324 set-in seams
 (p. 145)
sixteenths (p. 23)
design wall plan (p. 6)

yds.	Yardage or	fat qtrs.
3¾	cream prints	15
2¾	dark prints	11
2	med. prints	8
1	accent colors	4
½	binding	2
5¼	lining	25
	68" x 89" batting	

Cutting

cream prints for backgrounds
100 C: ☐ p. 16
25 strips 3½" x 18"
subcut 3½" squares

200 D: ◺ p. 16
20 strips 3" x 18"
subcut 3" squares
cut in half

112 E: ☐ p. 16
14 strips 2" x 18"
subcut 2" squares

112 F: ⊠ p. 16
6 strips 3⅜" x 18"
subcut 3⅜" squares
cut in half along both diagonals

30 G: ☐ p. 16
10 strips 5⅝" x 18"
subcut 5⅝" squares

dark prints for big/little stars (Y, Z)
border: (abutted)
18 strips 3+"* (*halfway
 between 3" and 3⅛")

312 A: ⟍45⟍ p. 17
52 strips 1½+"* x 18" (*halfway
 between 1½" and 1⅝")
45° angle
subcut 1½+"* diamonds

100 B: ⟍45⟍ p. 17
25 strips 1½+"* x 18" (*halfway

between 1½" and 1⅝")
45° angle
subcut 2⅝" parallelograms

medium prints for big stars (Y)
100 A: ⟍45⟍ p. 17
17 strips 1½+"* x 18" (*halfway
 between 1½" and 1⅝")
45° angle
subcut 1½+"* diamonds

100 B: ⟍45⟍ p. 17
25 strips 1½+"* x 18" (*halfway
 between 1½" and 1⅝")
45° angle
subcut 2⅝" parallelograms

34 H: ◿45⟍ p. 17
12 strips 4¼" x 18"
45° angle
subcut 6" parallelograms
cut in half to form 2 right triangles

4 I: ◺ p. 16
1 strip 4½" x 18"
subcut 4½" squares
cut in half diagonally

accent prints for little stars (Y, Z)
212 A: ⟍45⟍ p. 17
36 strips 1½+"* x 18" (*halfway
 between 1½" and 1⅝")
45° angle
subcut 1½+"* diamonds

candy-striped single binding
27 strips 1⅛" x 18"
45° angle
subcut random parallelograms

lining fabric
2 panels 34¼" x 89"

Successful Set-in Seams

Set-in joints are indicated in the diagrams by a pink dot. Don't sew from edge to edge of the patches at these joints. Start sewing at the end of the seamline, ¼" from the raw edge, at the set-in joint. Backtack exactly to the starting point. You will need to remove the work from the sewing machine to push seam allowances aside rather than pivoting at the angle.

Some people find it easier to start at the set-in point. That way, they can insert the needle at the proper point. If you have good control over your sewing machine, you can start at the other end and adjust the stitch to a very short stitch length as you near the end of the seam line in order to stop at the precise point desired. I usually put a pin at the end of the stitching line before I sew the seam. This tells me exactly where to stop. I pull the pin out just before it reaches the needle.

Most set-in situations involve two matching patches and one different one. I usually sew first one, then the other, of the matching patches to the different one. The final seam, then, is the one joining the two matching patches. Since these patches match, it is easier to align them perfectly for the final seam.

If you chain piece, you can modify your method for set-in patches. By starting at the opposite end of the seam from the set-in, you can begin stitching without lifting the presser foot. When you reach the end of the seam line, you will have to lift the presser foot and snip threads. While you have the presser foot up, insert the next unit, starting with the set-in point. Stitch from there to the edge of the patch at the opposite end. Do not lift the presser foot. Begin the next unit without lifting the presser foot. As you can see, by alternating ends you can chain stitch half of the time.

Construction

Make 50 Y units in 25 matched pairs. Make 28 Z units. Arrange the units, along with the G squares and H and I triangles as shown on page 146. If desired, Piece 'n' Play with the Z stars and plain G squares. Make diagonal rows and join them.

Join dark border strips to make 2 borders 80¼" long for sides and 2 borders 63⅝" long for top and bottom. Sew borders to sides, then top and bottom of quilt.

Mark the Wind Curls motif from page 141 in the G squares. Mark the chevrons from page 142 in the H and I triangles, extending the chevrons into the border. Make the binding from random-length parallelograms cut 1⅛" wide. Press seam allowances open after joining binding parallelograms. Bind to finish. (Note that this candy-striped binding, with its many seams, is the only binding in the book that is not double layered.)

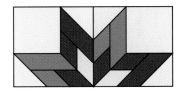

50 Y units

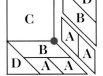

Y unit piecing

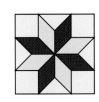

28 Z units

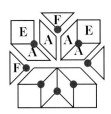

Z piecing

Quilting

Quilt Diagram

Judy's Fancy
Sleek & Scrappy

Designed by Judy Martin; made by Chris Hulin, 1999. Chris was trying to use up her scraps here, although she reports making as many as she used. Chris shifts background colors gradually from the upper left to lower right corners. Small stars are smattered randomly through the quilt, and the border is deleted. Chris substituted similar fabrics in many parts of the blocks for scrap nuance. The use of batiks and subtle color shifts makes Chris's quilt glow.

Quilt Size: 87" x 94¼"
Fits: queen bed
Unit Size: 10¼" x 5⅛"
Border Unit Size: 5⅛"
Requires:
98 Y units, 12 Z units
Cross References:
45° parallelograms (p. 17)
45° diamonds (p. 17)

¼ sq. triangles (p. 16)
squares (p. 16)
½ sq. triangles (p. 16)
45° triangles (p. 17)
292 set-in seams
  (p. 145)
sixteenths (p. 23)
fluid color (p. 6)
design wall plan (p. 6)

yds.	Yardage or	fat qtrs.
8	background	32
5¼	dk. star prints	21
¾	binding	3
8¾	lining	36
	91" x 99" batting	

Cutting

light background prints
196 C: ☐ **p. 16**
49 strips 3½" x 18"
subcut 3½" squares

392 D: ◻ **p. 16**
40 strips 3" x 18"
subcut 3" squares
cut in half

48 E: ☐ **p. 16**
6 strips 2" x 18"
subcut 2" squares

48 F: ⊠ **p. 16**
3 strips 3⅜" x 18"
subcut 3⅜" squares
cut in half along both diagonals

80 G: ☐ **p. 16**
27 strips 5⅝" x 18"
subcut 5⅝" squares

46 H: ◹ 45 **p. 17**
16 strips 4¼" x 18"
45° angle
subcut 6" parallelograms
cut in half to form 2 right triangles

4 I: ◺ **p. 16**
1 strip 4½" x 18"
subcut 4½" squares
cut in half diagonally

dark star prints
880 A: ▱ 45 **p. 17**
147 strips 1½+"* x 18"
  (*halfway between 1"
  and 1⅛")
45° angle
subcut 1½+"* diamonds

392 B: ▱ 45 **p. 17**
98 strips 1½+"* x 18"
45° angle
subcut 2⅝" parallelograms

folded binding
24 strips 2" x 18

lining fabric
3 panels 31" x 99"

*halfway between listed number and next higher ¹⁄₁₆"

Construction

Make 98 Y units in 49 matched pairs. Make 12 Z units. As you plan the units, arrange them on a design wall to achieve the effect of fluid color. Arrange the units, along with the G squares and H and I triangles as shown on page 149. Chris arranged her units with the warmest, lightest colors at the upper left and the darkest, coolest colors at the lower right.

Piece 'n' Play with the smattering of Z stars and plain G squares. Make diagonal rows and join them.

Mark concentric circles from page 83, centering the motif over each large star. Mark additional circles around the perimeter of the quilt to continue the pattern. Quilt as marked. Bind to finish.

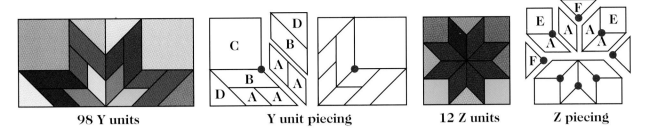

98 Y units **Y unit piecing** **12 Z units** **Z piecing**

Pink dots indicate set-in joints. See page 145 for detailed instructions.

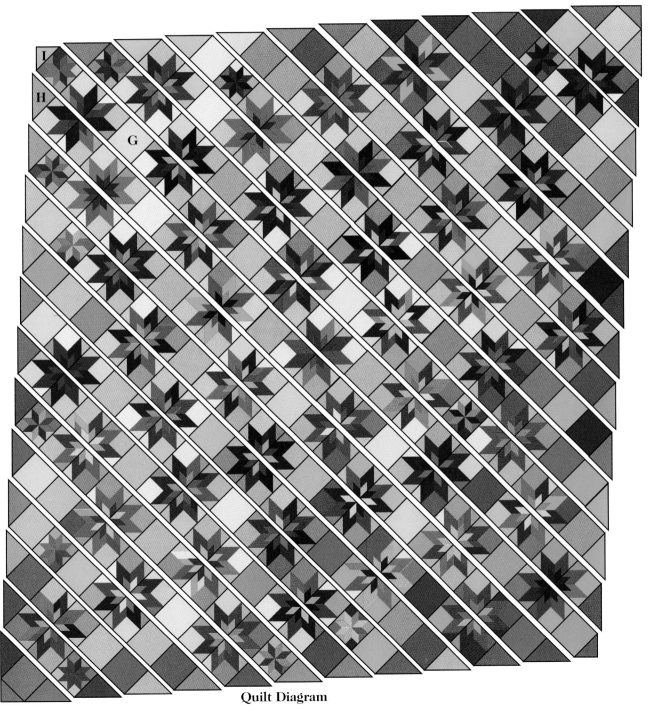

Quilt Diagram

Quilting

All Star

What Was I Thinking?

I loved the set of Judy's Fancy and wanted to come up with a design that would have a similar look but have no set-in or partial seams. I liked the idea of using a block with another motif superimposed over the center and then repeating the central motif in the small border blocks. Writer's Block, which I designed for *Judy Martin's Ultimate Book of Quilt Block Patterns,* was just such a block. A pinwheel motif embellishes a LeMoyne Star in this block. I split the background triangles to eliminate partial seams or set-ins and to enable me to make the quilt from uniform square units.

I first combined the Writer's Block variation with a Pinwheel block and the Judy's Fancy set in a Grand Block I made for *The Block Book.* This block, alone, makes a handsome wall quilt (page 159). I expanded on this idea, going back to the half block plan of Judy's Fancy, to make the Savannah in Summer version on page 154.

Quiltmaker's Style & Color Choices

The All Star wall quilt is a scrap quilt in a color scheme of lavender, purple, cream, and black. The queen-size version utilizes the same value placement, but the fabrics have busier prints and blocks are different colors. The queen-size quilt has quarter-block size plain squares of a slightly darker shade than the block backgrounds.

The wall quilt fabrics contrast highly with each other. Fabrics are current prints, mostly floral, and rather dainty. The queen-size quilt is made from vintage reproduction fabrics, including Savannah by Fons and Porter for Benartex and Civil War Prints by Judie Rothermel for Marcus Brothers. The queen-size quilt is softer focused than the crisp wall quilt. It has larger, busier prints, more colors, and lower contrasts. The warm prints suggest country, but the grand scale of some prints adds casual elegance.

Ideas For Taking All Star Further

For a slight change of rhythm, you can use the wall quilt version as a block. Make nine such 29" blocks and set them 3 x 3 for a queen-sized quilt or 2 x 3 for a twin quilt. This arrangement places accent pinwheels throughout the quilt in a regular pattern.

If you prefer to keep the pinwheels around the border, use the Judy's Fancy photo to help you plan the set for the twin-size All Star. The All Star and Judy's Fancy units are interchangeable, and the sets are the same design. The Judy's Fancy color scheme would work for All Star as well.

Try making All Star in red, black, cream, and gold as seen in Shakespeare in the Park on page 85. Or use a whimsical style and bright color scheme such as the Byzantine Flower Garden on page 170. Thirties prints or Japanese prints would also make lovely All Star quilts.

All Star is a good candidate for Piece 'n' Play. After making the units, play with their arrangement, sprinkling the pinwheels over the quilt in place of plain squares as desired.

Give All Star a contemporary look with fluid color, shifting values or hues from one area of the quilt to another. See Horn of Plenty on page 100 for an example.

Intersperse All Star blocks and Judy's Fancy blocks in the same quilt. Border with Pinwheels, LeMoyne Stars, or both.

Choose one color for the star points, another for background, and two others for pinwheels. Dance around these colors with a range of scrap fabrics. Mix up scrap fabrics within each block and from block to block.

Ideas to Be Gleaned From All Star

The large print and lower contrast busy style of the queen-size All Star would make a distinctive statement also in the Log Cabin and Virginia Reel patterns. The wide, printed border makes a dramatic statement.

Design your own original blocks by superimposing one block over another, as I have done with the Pinwheel and LeMoyne Star blocks to make All Star.

Use a smaller, related block as a border for any diagonally set quilt.

Color each block of a scrap quilt with its own set of fabrics. This is a fun way to play with your stash, and it lets you make this quilt piecemeal when you have a half hour here and there.

Cutting and Sewing Considerations

All Star simplifies the sewing of a LeMoyne Star by adding a pinwheel and eliminating the set-in seams.

The sewing unit here is a half block. You need to make matched pairs of half blocks, without sewing the halves together. Making half-blocks allows you to construct the quilt in simple rows, despite the staggered arrangement. When all units are made, arrange them according to the quilt diagram. Careful placement of matched units will yield whole blocks in the finished quilt.

The wide printed border on Savannah in Summer features an elegant partridge print. In order for the partridges to be right side up around three sides when the quilt was on the bed, I cut the borders crosswise. I then matched the print at the seams so the print continued without interruption. By placing a partridge motif at the center of each side, I was able to match the prints at the border corners of the square quilt. Partridge motifs and their reverses were printed in alternate rows on the fabric, so I cut two of each type and reversed direction at each corner of the quilt. This kind of fancy cutting takes extra yardage, but it makes the quilt a standout.

All Star

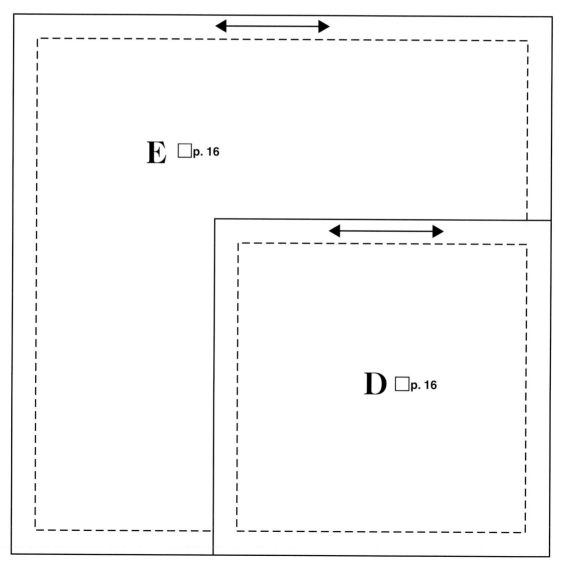

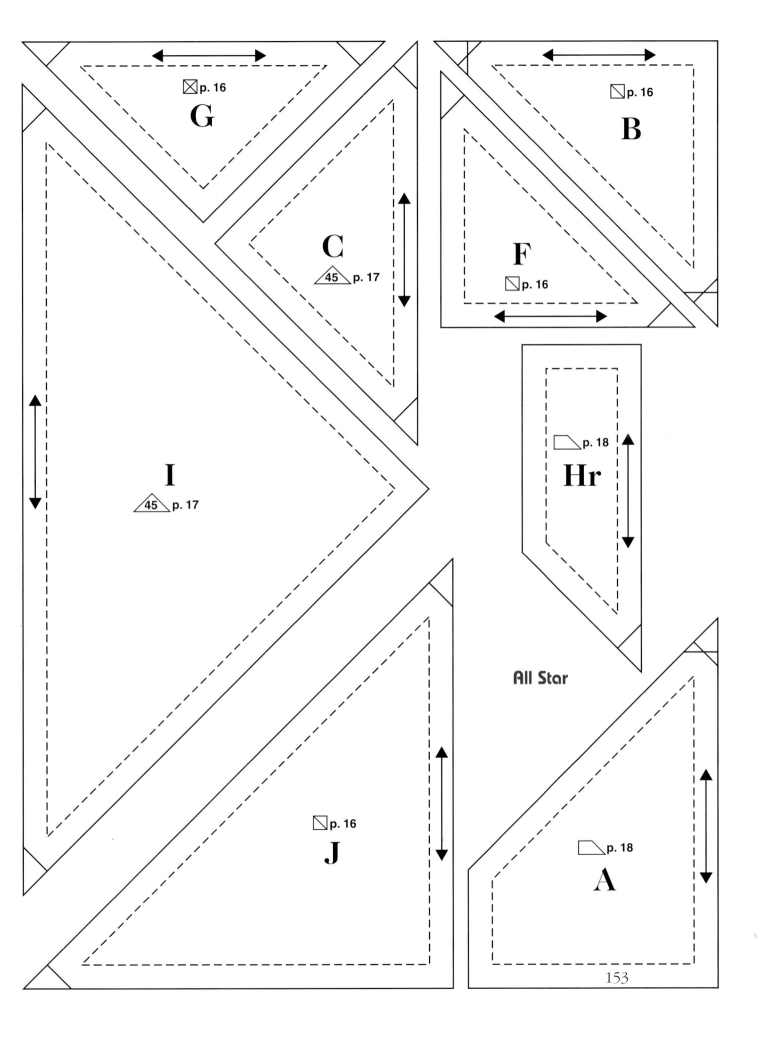

G ⊠ p. 16

B ◺ p. 16

C ◿45 p. 17

F ◿ p. 16

I ◿45 p. 17

Hr ▱ p. 18

J ◿ p. 16

A ▱ p. 18

All Star

153

All Star
Savannah in Summer

Designed and pieced by Judy Martin; quilted by Jean Nolte, 1999. For this quilt, I substituted two easier blocks for those in Judy's Fancy. No set-ins are needed here. A strong print in the wide borders and squares sets the tone in this quilt. Block backgrounds are somewhat lighter and less busy. Quilting is a simple grid pattern coupled with in-the-ditch quilting around the star details. Many of the fabrics are from Fons and Porter's Savannah line from Benartex and Judie Rothermel's Civil War prints from Marcus Brothers. Batting is 100% cotton with scrim by Hobbs.

Quilt Size: 83½" x 83½"
Fits: double/queen bed
Unit Size: 10¼" x 5⅛"
Border Unit Size: 5⅛"
Requires:
58 Y units
29 Z border units
Cross References:
½ sq. triangles (p. 16)

¼ sq. triangles (p. 16)
squares (p. 16)
½ trapezoids (p. 18)
reversals (p. 22)
45° triangles (p. 17)
sixteenths (p. 23)
4 set-ins optional for
  borders (p. 145)
design wall plan (p. 6)

Yardage			
yds.		**or**	**fat qtrs.**
3¾	cream prints		15
2¾	camel print		11
1¾	medium prints		7
2¼*	dark prints		*9

(*1½ yds. or 6 fat qtrs. if you use S45 tool)

1	brights	4
¾	binding	3
7¾	lining	30

88" x 88" batting

Cutting

cream prints for background
232 B: ◻p. 16
24 strips 3" x 18"
subcut 3" squares
cut in half diagonally

116 D: ☐p. 16
29 strips 3½" x 18"
subcut 3½" squares

116 G: ⊠p. 16
8 strips 3¾+"* x 18" (*halfway
  between 3¾" and 3⅞")
subcut 3¾+"* squares (*halfway
  between 3¾" and 3⅞")
cut in half along both diagonals

116 Hr: (fabric face down) ◻p. 18
29 strips 1¼" x 18"
subcut 3⅜+"* rectangles (*halfway
  between 3⅜" and 3½")
cut off end at 45° angle

7 E: ☐p. 16
3 strips 5⅝" x 18"
subcut 5⅝" squares

dark prints for star points (Y)
232 A: ◻p. 18
58* strips 2⅝" x 18"
  *39 strips if using S45 tool
subcut 3⅞" rectangles
cut off end at 45° angle

folded binding
22 strips 2" x 18"

medium prints for pinwheels (Y, Z)
116 B: ◻p. 16
12 strips 3" x 18"
subcut 3" squares
cut in half diagonally

116 F: ◻p. 16
10 strips 2⅝+"* x 18" (*halfway
  between 2⅝" and 2¾")
subcut 2⅝+"* squares (*halfway
  between 2⅝" and 2¾")
cut in half diagonally

36 I: ◺45◹p. 17
12 strips 4¼" x 18"
45° angle
subcut 6" parallelograms
cut in half diagonally to form
  2 right triangles

4 J: ◻p. 16
1 strip 4½" x 18"
subcut 4½" squares
cut in half diagonally

camel print for border, squares
border: (mitered)
4 strips 6" x 84¾"

29 E: ☐p. 16
10 strips 5⅝" x 18"
subcut 5⅝" squares

lining fabric
3 panels 29½" x 87½"

bright prints for pinwheels (Y, Z)
116 C: ⟋45⟍ p. 17
17 strips 2⅛" x 18"
45° angle
subcut 3" parallelograms
cut in half to form 2 right
triangles

116 G: ⊠ p. 16
8 strips 3¾+"* x 18" (*halfway
between 3¾" and 3⅞")
subcut 3¾+"* squares (*halfway
between 3¾" and 3⅞")
cut in half along both
diagonals

A Bias Approach

The bias can stretch, but this is no reason to be intimidated. A few basic precautions will have you handling the bias like a pro. Quilters have devised countless detours to avoid bias edges. What they may not realize is that bias doesn't need to be cut in order to stretch. Improper handling can stretch bias whether the edge is cut or not. For perfect results, follow these simple guidelines.

1. Plan patch cutting so the straight grain of the fabric falls around the edges of blocks and units. (The cutting directions for each pattern in the book do it for you.) Not until all bias edges are stitched down should you press the unit.

2. As you rotary cut along the bias, hold the ruler extra firmly near the points of the patch. Don't let the fabric be pulled out from under the ruler at the point, or you may end up with some distortion. A sharp blade is helpful to avoid pulling the fabric. Of course, be sure to keep your fingertips out of the path of the rotary cutter!

3. As you feed patches into the sewing machine, hold them flat against the sewing machine bed. If the entire patch is flat, it cannot be stretched. Don't hold the fabric between your thumb and index finger after it reaches the machine bed. Instead, simply let your hands float over the fabric, keeping it flat at the seam line and clear off to the side of the seam. Don't push or pull the fabric, just guide it gently.

4. Pin long seams, such as borders, at regular intervals. Keep the work supported on a flat surface, such as a table or bed, as you pin.

5. Fingerpress units, rather than pressing or ironing, until the bias edges have been stitched. Then use a dry iron instead of steam and press (without moving the iron back and forth) or iron with the iron moving back and forth in the direction of the straight grain.

Construction

Note that B and C patches are the same size but different colors and grains. F and G are also the same size but different colors and grains. Pay attention to the colors in the diagrams, and remember that the straight grain goes around the edges of the units.

Make 58 Y units in 29 matched pairs. Make 29 Z units. Arrange these units with the E squares and I and J triangles in diagonal rows as shown on the facing page. Make rows and join them.

Add borders. (I seamed crosswise strips together, matching the print at the seams, to make the partridge print border as shown. Usually, I cut lengthwise borders, but with this particular fabric that would have resulted in sideways birds around the border. Adjust the width of your border to the print or quilting motif, if desired.)

See the quilting diagram on page 158. Quilt in the ditch around all patches. Quilt lines dividing the E squares in quarters. Extend these lines through the edge triangles and border. Bind to finish.

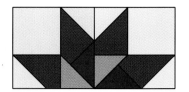

58 Y units

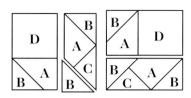

Y unit piecing

29 Z units

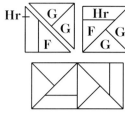

Z unit piecing

Quilt Diagram

157

Quilting

All Star
Pretty Posies

 Designed and made by Judy Martin; quilted by Jean Nolte, 1998. Dainty florals create a softer, more delicate look in this version. Backgrounds are more uniform, and each scrap block repeats the same color scheme. A smattering of small pinwheel blocks creates a built-in border. This quilt is assembled from half-block rows on the diagonal. It is helpful to arrange half blocks and other units on a design wall or floor before making the rows. The quilting pattern of tendrils featured here is more elaborate than the simple grid in the Savannah in Summer variation.

All Star: Pretty Posies

Quilt Size: 29" x 29"
Fits: wall
Unit Size: 10¼" x 5⅛"
Border Unit Size: 5⅛"
Requires:
8 Y units
8 Z units

Cross References:
¼ sq. triangles (p. 16)
½ sq. triangles (p. 16)
squares (p. 16)
½ trapezoids (p. 18)
45° triangles (p. 17)
reversals (p. 22)
sixteenths (p. 23)
design wall plan (p. 6)

Yardage		
yds.	or	fat qtrs.
1¼	creams	5
¼	purples	1
¼	lavenders	1
⅜	blacks	2
¼	binding	1
1	lining	4
33" x 33" batting		

cream prints

32 B: ◻p. 16
4 strips 3" x 18"
subcut 3" squares
cut in half diagonally

16 D: ◻p. 16
4 strips 3½" x 18"
subcut 3½" squares

1 E: ◻p. 16
1 square 5⅝" x 5⅝"

32 G: ⊠p. 16
2 strips 3¾+"* x 18" (*halfway
   between 3¾" and 3⅞")
subcut 3¾+"* squares
cut in half along both diagonals

32 Hr: (fabric face down) ◻p. 18
8 strips 1¼" x 18"
subcut 3⅜+"* rectangles (*halfway
   between 3⅜" and 3½")
cut off end at 45° angle

12 I: ◁45◁ p. 17
4 strips 4¼" x 18"
45° angle
subcut 6" parallelograms
cut in half to form 2 right triangles

4 J: ◻p. 16
1 strip 4½" x 18"
subcut 4½" squares
cut in half diagonally

folded binding
8 strips 2" x 18"

purple prints

16 C: ◁45◁ p. 17
3 strips 2⅛" x 18"
45° angle
subcut 3" parallelograms
cut in half to form 2 right
   triangles

32 G: ⊠p. 16
2 strips 3¾+"* x 18" (*halfway
   between 3¾" and 3⅞")
subcut 3¾+"* squares
cut in half along both diagonals

lavender prints

16 B: ◻p. 16
2 strips 3" x 18"
subcut 3" squares
cut in half diagonally

32 F: ◻p. 16
3 strips 2⅝+"* x 18" (*halfway
   between 2⅝" and 2¾")
subcut 2⅝+"* squares
cut in half diagonally

black prints
32 A: ◻p. 18
8 strips 2⅝" x 18"
subcut 3⅞" rectangles
cut off end at 45° angle

lining fabric
1 panel 33" x 33"

Make 8 Y units in 4 matched pairs. Make 8 Z units. Arrange these units with the E square and I and J triangles in diagonal rows as shown on the facing page. Make rows and join them.

Mark the pink curl from the quilting motif on page 162 in the I triangles. Mark the entire black and pink motif from page 162 in the E square, extending onto the neighboring blocks. Quilt as marked and quilt in the ditch around all patches. Bind to finish. Don't forget to sign and date your quilt.

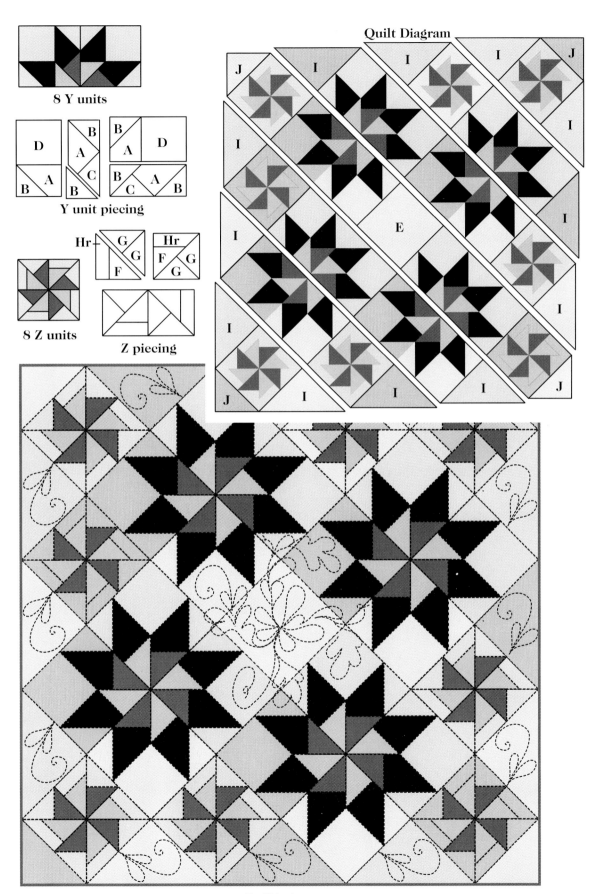

8 Y units

Y unit piecing

8 Z units

Z piecing

Quilt Diagram

Quilting

Curlicue quilting

Byzantine Flower Garden

What Was I Thinking?

This pattern was inspired by the Grandmother's Flower Garden pattern that was so very popular during the Great Depression. Those quilts often featured hexagons fancy cut to center the print. I wanted to preserve that look. I also wanted to simplify the pattern for machine piecing, and embellish it with my signature, stars.

Quiltmaker's Style & Color Choices

My Prints on Parade version is interpreted in nineteenth century reproduction prints and colors. Each block is made from a set of three fabrics: a light, a medium, and a dark. Star points are always medium or dark; hexagons can be any value; backgrounds are always light or medium. I used fancy cutting in the hexagons and a few of the diamonds for a lacy look. The quilting is correspondingly formal, with elegant sprigs.

My Wild Whimsy version has a jaunty, youthful, contemporary feel. The brilliant colors and quirky prints are playful. This quilt also employs fancy cutting, this time to show off the brightly colored turtles in the green print. The quilting in this version is simpler and more casual.

Ideas for Taking
Byzantine Flower Garden Further

For a twin-sized quilt, make 14 rows of 5 units. Pieced side borders will be the same as those for the queen-sized quilt. Top and bottom borders each require 7 fewer border units. The length and width of the inner borders will need to be adjusted to fit.

The color scheme from Acrobatik on page 90 would be attractive in Byzantine Flower Garden. The color scheme from Grandmother's Wedding Ring on page 50 would also be suitable.

Try using a gradated background print such as that in Grandmother's Wedding Ring on page 38.

Byzantine Flower Garden would look absolutely right in a '30s style with pastels and muslin. See the Grandmother's Diamond Ring quilt on page 54. Amish or Japanese styles would also be stunning.

This quilt can be streamlined by eliminating the fancy cutting for the hexagons. Byzantine Flower Garden is beautiful any way you cut it.

Ideas to Be Gleaned From
Byzantine Flower Garden

The Wild Whimsy version offers a good way to quilt a busy print border: simply extend the lines from the adjacent pieced border. Elaborate quilting won't show up on a busy print, but the border still needs some kind of quilting.

The daisy quilting in the Wild Whimsy stars will enhance just about any 6-pointed star. I show it in the diagrams for the Horn of Plenty quilts (pages 103 and 107).

The small stipple quilting in the light inner border of both quilts is an excellent alternative to a grid of squares. Squares can look out of place on a quilt of 60° shapes, but you still need filler quilting to make the other areas puff up nicely to show off their details. Stippling serves this purpose well.

The vintage style of one Byzantine Flower Garden and the whimsical style of the other offer excellent models for varied scrap quilt styles. Apply their color schemes and fabric choices to many different quilts. The Grandmother's Wedding Ring and Texas Chain quilts would be perfect candidates.

Fancy cutting accentuates the patches and calls attention to the prints for a totally different look. In fact, the look varies depending on the print. Try it on any quilt.

Cutting & Sewing Considerations

My star in the center of the block naturally divides the block into six wedges. Background triangles fill in around the hexagons for straight block edges and easy sewing without set-ins or paper piecing.

Fancy-cut hexagons ring the central star. Fancy cutting gives you special effects, and it can be done with a rotary cutter. See my help box on page 172. Note that fancy cutting takes additional yardage.

The construction unit is half of the hexagonal block. By making half-block units, you can assemble the quilt in easy rows.

163

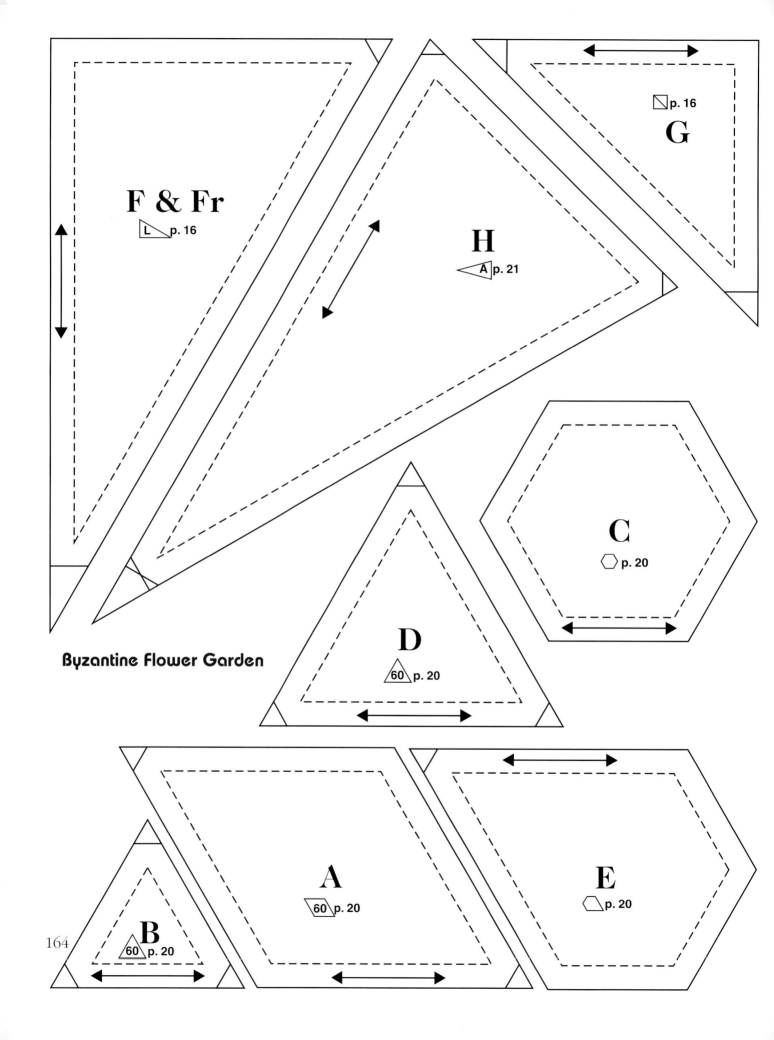

F & Fr

L ◁ p. 16

H

◁ A p. 21

G

☐ p. 16

C

⬡ p. 20

D

△ 60 p. 20

Byzantine Flower Garden

A

◇ 60 p. 20

B

△ 60 p. 20

E

⬡ p. 20

Byzantine Flower Garden
Prints on Parade

Designed and pieced by Judy Martin; quilted by Jean Nolte, 1999. This quilt has a Grandmother's Flower Garden look without the set-in seams and without paper piecing. It can be easily rotary cut and machine pieced without paper foundations. Hexagons in all of the blocks, diamonds in a few, and clipped diamonds in the border were rotary cut precisely centered over printed motifs. This gives the quilt its lacy quality. Blocks with light hexagons and those with darker hexagons are arranged in a regular pattern, subtly echoing the traditional arrangement of six hexagons around a contrasting center. The wide border is quilted with leafy sprigs, and the blocks are quilted in the ditch. This quilt is made from half-block rows. Batting is 100% cotton with scrim by Hobbs.

Quilt Size: 90⅛" x 97"
Fits: queen bed
Unit Size: 5" high x
  11.54" wide
Set: 14 rows of 7 units
Requires:
78 Y, 20 Z
Cross References:
60° diamonds (p. 20)

hexagons (p. 20)
60° triangles (p. 20)
clipped diamonds (p. 20)
long triangles (p. 16)
acute triangles (p. 21)
½ sq. triangles (p. 16)
fancy cutting (p. 172)
reversals (p. 22)
sixteenths (p. 23)

	Yardage	
yds.	or	fat qtrs.
3	dark prints	12
4¾	medium prints	19
3¾	light prints	15
2⅞	green border	12
1	light accent	4
¾	binding	3
9	lining	36
94" x 101" batting		

Cutting

dark prints for diamonds
424 A: \60\ **p. 20**
85 strips 2½" x 18"
60° angle
subcut 2½" diamonds

medium prints
border: (abutted)
9 strips 2¾+"* x 18" (sides)
  (*halfway between 2¾" and 2⅞")
9 strips 3" x 18" (top/bottom)

1292 B: /60\ **p. 20**
86 strips 1¾" x 18"
60° angle
subcut 1¾" diamonds
cut in half

120 C: ⬡ **p. 20**
24 strips 2½" x 18"
60° angle
subcut 2½" diamonds
subcut 1¼" from diagonal midline
subcut 2½" from edge

134 D: /60\ **p. 20**
15 strips 2¾" x 18"
60° angle
subcut 2¾" diamonds
cut in half

14 F: L **p. 16**
4 strips 3½+"* x 18" (*halfway
  between 3½" and 3⅝")

subcut 6⅛+"* rectangles (*halfway
  between 6⅛" and 6¼")
cut in half diagonally

14 Fr: (fabric face down) L **p. 16**
4 strips 3½+"* x 18" (*halfway
  between 3½" and 3⅝")
subcut 6⅛+"* rectangles (*halfway
  between 6⅛" and 6¼")
cut in half diagonally

4 G: ◪ **p. 16**
1 strip 3" x 18"
subcut 3" squares
cut in half diagonally

light prints
300 B: /60\ **p. 20**
20 strips 1¾" x 18" 60° angle
subcut 1¾" diamonds
cut in half

468 C: ⬡ **p. 20**
94 strips 2½" x 18"
60° angle
subcut 2½" diamonds
subcut 1¼" from diagonal midline
subcut 2½" from edge

green prints for border
border:
24 strips 6½" x 18"

light accent print in pieced border

126 E: ⬜\p. 20
26 strips 2½" x 18"
60° angle
subcut 2½" diamonds
subcut 1¼" from diagonal midline

4 H: ◁A\p. 21
2 strips 3½" x 18"
trim off 60° at end of strip

subcut 3½" diamond
cut in half diagonally

folded binding
24 strips 2" x 18"

lining fabric
3 panels 32" x 101"

Construction

Make 78 Y and 20 Z units in matched pairs. Make 14 rows of 7, adding 1 F and 1 Fr to opposite ends of each. Join rows.

Join 2¾+" border strips to make 2 borders 70½" long; sew to sides. Join 3" strips to make 2 borders of 68⅝"; sew to top/bottom.

Make 122 pieced border units and 4 end units. For each side border, join 32 border units and 1 end unit. For each top/bottom border, join 29 border units and 1 end unit. Sew a G to each H. Sew one of these to each end of top and bottom borders. Sew pieced borders to quilt. Miter corners (p. 145).

Join green strips to make 2 side borders 85½" long and 2 top/bottom borders 90⅝" long. Attach side, then top/bottom borders.

Mark and quilt the sprig motifs from page 169 in the outer borders. Quilt in the ditch around diamonds, hexagons, and clipped diamonds. Stipple quilt the medium borders and F and Fr triangles. Bind to finish. Sign your quilt and enjoy sweet dreams under it!

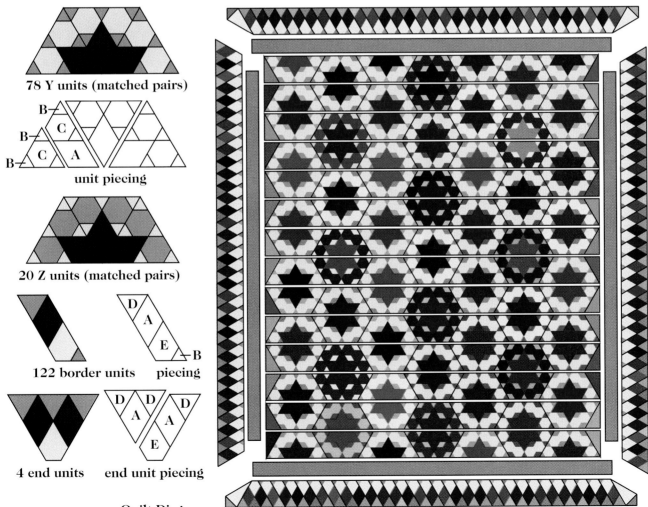

78 Y units (matched pairs)

unit piecing

20 Z units (matched pairs)

122 border units   **piecing**

4 end units   **end unit piecing**

Quilt Diagram

Quilting

Border Corner Motif

Border quilting, 2 repeats

Border Motif

169

Byzantine Flower Garden
Wild Whimsy

Designed and pieced by Judy Martin; quilted by Jean Nolte, 1999. Clipped diamonds in the pieced border and hexagons in a few blocks are carefully cut to center the turtle figures in the print. In this case, cutting in strips wasted too many turtle motifs, so I cut shapes using templates. Centering the print makes a busy print orderly. The print borders are quilted in simple parallel lines, as a motif would not show up well. Diamond patches are quilted with a Daisy pattern. The turtle print is from K.P. Kids by South Seas Imports. Batting is 100% cotton with scrim by Hobbs.

Quilt Size: 49⅝" x 61"
Fits: crib, wall or throw
Unit Size: 5" high x
  11.54" wide
Set: 8 rows of 3 units
Requires:
14 Y, 10 Z
Cross References:
60° diamonds (p. 20)

hexagons (p. 20)
60° triangles (p. 20)
clipped diamonds (p. 20)
long triangles (p. 16)
acute triangles (p. 21)
½ sq. triangles (p. 16)
fancy cutting (p. 172)
reversals (p. 22)
sixteenths (p. 23)

yds.	Yardage or	fat qtrs.
2⅛	green print	8
1¾	background	7
1¾	bright prints	7
½	binding	2
3⅞	lining	16
	54" x 65" batting	

Cutting

green print
border: (abutted)
cut off a 56" x 45" piece and cut:
2 strips 3½" x 55½" (sides)
2 strips 3½" x 50⅛" (top/bottom)

cut all remaining green print into
4 lengths of about 18" and cut:

60 C: ⬡ **p. 20**
12 strips 2½" x 18"
60° angle
subcut 2½" diamonds
subcut 1¼" from diagonal midline
subcut 2½" from edge

70 E: ◁ **p. 20**
14 strips 2½" x 18"
60° angle
subcut 2½" diamonds
subcut 1¼" from diagonal midline

4 H: ◁A **p. 21**
2 strips 3½" x 18"
trim off 60° at end of strip
subcut 3½" diamond
cut in half diagonally

light background print or solid
cut off a 40½" length and cut:

border: (abutted)
2 strips 2⅞" x 40½" (sides)
2 strips 3" x 34" (top/bottom)

cut all remaining light green print into
  3 lengths of 18" and cut:

426 B: △60 **p. 20**
27 strips 1¾" x 18"
60° angle
subcut 1¾" diamonds
cut in half

78 D: △60 **p. 20**
8 strips 2¾" x 18"
60° angle
subcut 2¾" diamonds
cut in half

4 G: ◻ **p. 16**
1 strip 3" x 18"
subcut 3" squares
cut in half diagonally

8 F: L◣ **p. 16**
2 strips 3½+"* x 18"
  (*halfway between
  3½" and 3⅝")
subcut 6⅛+"* rectangles (*halfway
  between 6⅛" and 6¼")
cut in half diagonally

8 Fr: (fabric face down) L◢ **p. 16**
2 strips 3½"+* x 18"
  (*halfway between 3½" and 3⅝")
subcut 6⅛+"* rectangles
  (*halfway between 6⅛" and 6¼")
cut in half diagonally

bright prints
146 A: \60\ p. 20
30 strips 2½" x 18"
60° angle
subcut 2½" diamonds

84 C: ⬡ p. 20
17 strips 2½" x 18"
60° angle
subcut 2½" diamonds

subcut 1¼" from diagonal midline
subcut 2½" from edge

folded binding
15 strips 2" x 18"

lining fabric
2 panels 27" x 65"

Fancy Cutting for Special Effects

You can fancy cut a diamond or hexagon to center a printed motif in it for a special look. See Figure 1, below. Find the center of the motif. Lay the rule line for *half* the strip width over the centers of each motif in a row. Cut the strip.

See Fig. 2. Measure the full strip width from the edge you just cut, and cut again to complete the strip.

See Fig. 3. Lay your half-strip measurement over the motif center, and place the 60° line even with the base of the strip. Cut the first side of the diamond.

See Fig. 4. Rotate the strip. Now cut a diamond or hexagon as usual.

There will probably be waste between strips and between diamonds, so you'll need extra yardage for fancy cutting.

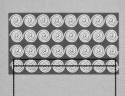

Fig. 1
center rule line
over motifs
and cut strip

Fig. 2
measure strip
from 1st cut
and trim strip

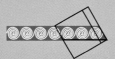

Fig. 3
cut 60° angle
with motif centered

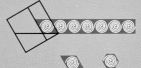

Fig. 4
complete the
shape as usual

Construction

Make 24 units in matched pairs. Make 8 rows of 3 units, as shown, adding F to one end and Fr to the other end. Join rows.

Add the light side borders, then add the shorter top and bottom borders. Join 19 border units and 1 end unit. Attach to side. Repeat for opposite side. Join 14 border units and 1 end unit. Sew to top. Repeat for bottom. Miter corners (p. 145).

Add green side borders, then add top and bottom borders.

Mark and quilt the Daisy motif from page 174 in the stars. Quilt in the ditch around diamonds, hexagons, and clipped diamonds. Extend the quilting lines through the outer borders. Stipple quilt the light borders and F and Fr triangles. Bind to finish. Sign and date your quilt with pride.

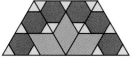

14 Y units

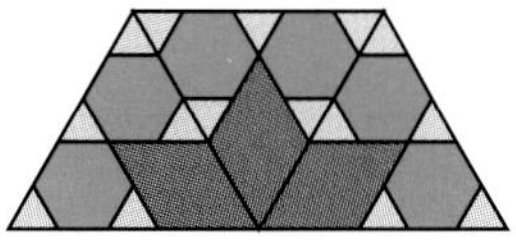

10 Z units

unit piecing

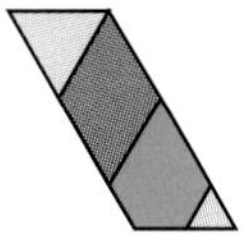

66 border units

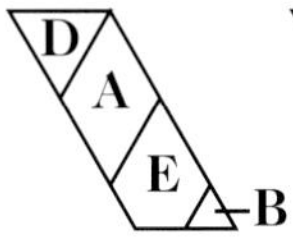

piecing

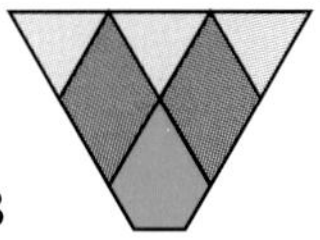

4 end units

end unit piecing

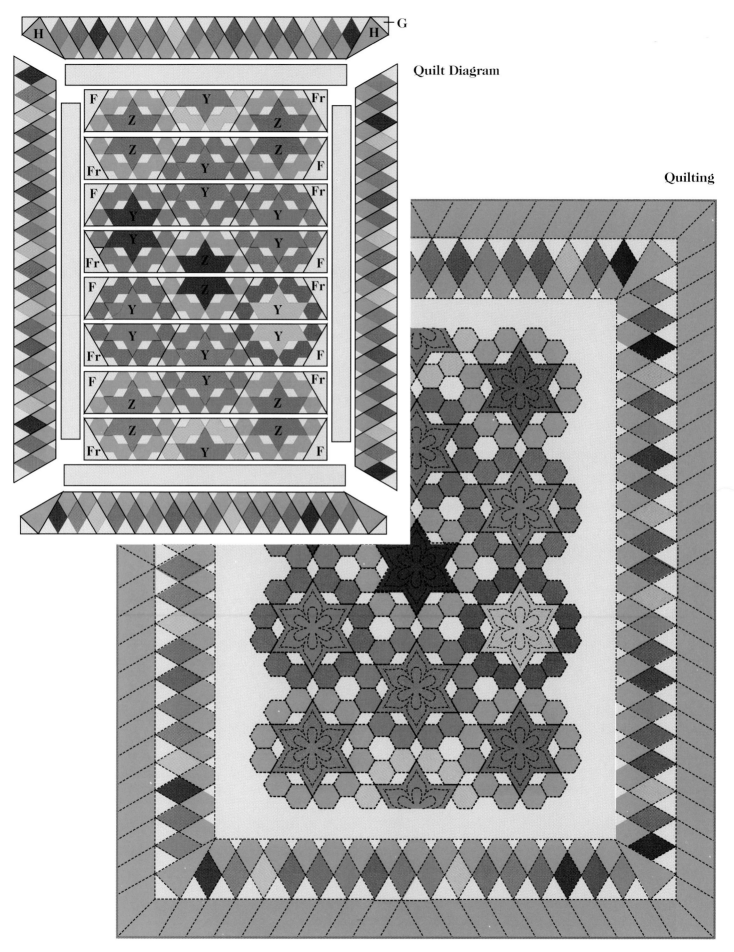

Quilt Diagram

Quilting

Daisy quilting motif

Index of Topics

Index of Patterns

Sources

**Quilting with Judy Martin:
the Site Dedicated to Empowering Quilters
http://www.judymartin.com**

secure online ordering
copyright and permission details
teacher guidelines and class outlines
answers to frequently asked questions
gallery of reader quilts from Judy's books
information on the latest fabrics
free block of the month
lessons on topics such as:
   how to cut diamonds & parallelograms
   how to make a 2:1 angle on your ruler
   how to make binding

▼▲▼▲▼▲▼▲▼▲▼▲▼▲▼

**Watch for *Piece 'n' Play Quilts*
by Judy Martin in 2001.**

Do You Have These Judy Martin Books?

The Block Book: 174 block patterns, new blocks, Grand Blocks, and more.

Judy Martin's Ultimate Rotary Cutting Reference: yardage figures for all shapes and sizes, rotary cutting helps, tool use, more.

Pieced Borders by Judy Martin & Marsha McCloskey: 200 border patterns, border techniques, 12 complete quilt patterns.

And These Great Tools?

Rotaruler 16 (R16)
Point Trimmer (PT)
Shapemaker 45 (S45)

▼▲▼▲▼▲▼▲▼▲▼▲▼▲▼

Look for them at your favorite quilt shops or order direct at 1-800-642-5615